AMER

RECIPES

A Complete Cookbook of Us Dish Ideas!

(Easy, Healthy and Delicious American Recipes for Beginners)

Betty Sullivan

Published by Sharon Lohan

© **Betty Sullivan**

American Recipes: A Complete Cookbook of Us Dish Ideas! (Easy, Healthy and Delicious American Recipes for Beginners)

ISBN 978-1-7776245-3-8

Legal & Disclaimer

The information contained in this book is not designed to replace or take the place of any form of medicine or professional medical advice. The information in this book has been provided for educational and entertainment purposes only.

Table of contents

Part 1...1

Introduction 2

Fried Chicken Waffles...3

Smoked Salmon Breakfast Crackers...6

Apricot Ricotta Bagels 8

Kale Slaw With Hazelnut Dressing...10

Grilled Fruit Skewers 12

Sriracha And Cheddar Burgers...14

Mini Macs...16

Cheesy Jalapeno Pretzel Bites...19

Boneless Buffalo Wings...22

Grilled Cheese Burger...24

Blue Cheese Burgers...26

Dark Chocolate Brownies 28

Lemon Tart...30

White Chocolate Muffins 32

Basic Buttermilk Waffles...34

Pecan Pie 36

Triple Chocolate Cookies...39

White Chocolate Blueberry Tart...41

White Chocolate Blondies...44

Grilled Wings + Sauce 46

Basic Soft Pretzels...48

Ribs 50

Nyc Street Hotdogs..52

Candy Apple | Enchanted 54

Corn Dogs | Princess Diaries 56

Nyc Pizza 58

Hot Chocolate..61

Hawaiian Punch..63

Shrimp Tacos With Tomatillo Black Bean Salsa....................65

Tex-Mex Chipotle Beans 67

Conclusion...69

Part 2...70

Latin American Recipes 71

1. Mixed Squash Tacos..71

2. Chipotle Chicken And Corn Tostadas 72

3. Grilled Steak Skewers With Arugula Chimichuri.................74

4. Seafood Guacamole 76

5. Grilled Chicken With Curried Couscous, Spinach And Mango
....78

6. Pernil-Style Beef Tenderloin 80

7. Black Pepper Crusted Beef Tenderloin With Chimichurri Sauce 82

8. Poblano And Ham Quesadillas......84

9. Siloin Tacos 85

10. Steak Adobo 87

11. Chicken Fajitas With Red Pepper, Onion And Lime......88

12. Classic Pico De Gallo 90

13. Migas (Scrambled Eggs With Corn Tortillas)......91

14. Avocado, Mango And Pineapple Salad With Pistachios And Pickled Shallots......93

15. Spicy Grilled Corn Salad With Black Beans And Queso Fresco 95

16. Cube Steak With Lime Mojo 97

17. Breakfast Burrito......99

18. Spicy Cilantro Chicken Wings......101

19. Smoky Corn Quesadillas 103

20. Black Pepper Crusted Beef Tenderloin With Chimichurri Sauce 104

21. Seared Tilapia With Spicy Orange Salsa......106

22. Brazilian Skirt Steak With Golden Garlic Butter 108

23. Grilled Steak Tacos With Spicy Slaw......109

24. Grilled Portobello Quesadillas 111

25. Grilled Chicken With Curried Couscous, Spinach And Mango......113

26. Sofrito Scallops With Saffron Rice 115

27. Spinach And Tomatilla Guacamole 117

28. Tomatillo Gazpacho 118

29. Southwestern Rice Pilaf 120

30. Grilled Chicken With Tomato, Lime And Cilantro Salsa 122

Roasted Pork Loin 124

Steaks – Portuguese Style 125

Country: Brazil 125

Lemon Chimichurri 126

Famous Meat-Filled Empanadas 126

Potato Cake Recipe – LLapingachos 128

Valdiviano (Beef Jerky And Onion Soup) 130

Tomatican Con Pulpa De Cerdo (Corn And Pork Stew) 131

Spicy Crab Cakes 132

Pastel De Zapallitos 133

Shrimp And Fish Stew 134

Peruvian Garlic Chicken 135

Pork With Lemon 137

Garlic Pork 138

Pepperpot 139

Yum-Yums 140

Breadfruit Cheese Pie 141

Stuffed Zucchini (Zapallitos Rellenos) 142

Croquetas de Atún – Tuna Croquettes..................143

Crema de Apio – Celery Root Soup..................145

Country: Venezuela..................146

Jalapeño Tequeño Poppers..................147

Egg Ball..................149

Mango Sours..................150

Main Recipes..................151

Buffalo Chicken and Rice Skillet..................151

Baked Chicken with Mustard and Lime..................152

Black Bean and Guac Burritos..................153

Rosemary Rubbed Rib-Eye Steak Recipe..................154

Parmesan Crusted Chicken..................155

Chipotle Popcorn Chicken..................157

Chicago Chicken..................157

Revolutionary Mac and Cheese..................158

Melt in your Mouth Chicken..................159

Ham and Cheese Breakfast Sandwich with Mango Chutney..................160

Pumpkin Chocolate Waffles..................161

New York Classic Breakfast Chip..................162

Best Breakfast Pancakes..................164

Southern Sausage Gravy..................165

Orange Scented Mocha..................166

Snickers Cheesecake...167

Applesauce Pie 168

Southern Sweet Potato Pie Recipe......................................169

Southern Peach Cobbler 170

Buffalo Chicken Wings...171

Bruschetta-Goat Cheese Cups 173

Caramelized Onion-Apple Bites..173

Southwest Bean Dip...175

Southern Fried Dill Pickles...175

Disappearing Buffalo Chicken Dip..176

Kale Slaw with Apples, Cranberries and Creamy Maple.......177

Cranberry Almond Coleslaw 178

Apple Cranberry Walnut Salad...179

Southern Chicken Salad 180

Summer Corn Salad 181

Sweet Cabbage Salad 182

Carrot cake pancakes...183

Meatball Sliders 184

Banana Oreo Milkshake...185

Part 1

Introduction

Who doesn't love American food! An all round crowd pleaser, the American cuisine is full of favorites. From deep fried golden goodness to yummy breakfast options, and all time favorite desserts, this recipe book is full of classics we all enjoy.

Almost all the recipes in this book can be easily doubled or tripled as needed. Each recipe includes simple ingredients and step-by-step instructions that ensures guaranteed deliciousness. So, what are you waiting for? Let's get started!

Fried Chicken Waffles

Crispy, crunchy, sweet, and savory? This is the epitome of an American dish! These fried chicken waffles are the perfect appetizer for a large party.

Total Time: 40m

Servings: 24

Ingredients:

For chicken

- Canola oil and for frying
- 1 ¼ cups of all-purpose flour
- 2 Tbsp. of cornstarch
- 1 tsp. of cayenne pepper
- 1 Tbsp. of dried Italian seasoning
- 2 tsp. of salt
- 1 tsp. of black pepper
- 1 cup of buttermilk
- 1 ½ lb. chicken tenders, cut into small pieces
- Hot sauce, for serving

3

For Waffles

- 2 tsp. of yeast
- ½ cup of warm water
- 1 ¾ cup of whole milk
- 6 Tbsp. of butter, melted
- 2 eggs
- ½ tsp. of pure vanilla
- 2 cups of all-purpose flour
- 1 Tbsp. of white sugar
- Dash of salt
- Dash of cinnamon powder

Waffle Topping

- 1 cup sugar
- 2 tbsp. powdered cinnamon

Directions:

Prepare the waffles. In a bowl, combine yeast and warm water. Stir well to mix. Set aside to rest for 5 minutes or foamy.

In a separate bowl, add in the whole milk, melted butter, eggs and pure vanilla. Whisk light to mix. Add into the yeast mix.

In a different bowl, add flour, white sugar, dash of salt and powdered cinnamon. Stir to mix. Add into the milk mixture. Whisk well until smooth in consistency.

Cover and chill overnight.

4

Preheat a waffle iron. Grease with cooking spray.

Pour ¼ cup of the waffle batter onto the iron. Close the lid and cook for 5 minutes or until golden. Remove and repeat.

In a bowl, add in the cinnamon and white sugar for the topping. Stir well to mix. Toss the waffles with the topping until coated on all sides. Place onto a wire rack to rest.

In a pot on med heat, add 3 inches of canola oil. Heat the oil until it reaches 350 degrees.

Prepare the chicken. In a bowl, add the flour, cayenne pepper, dried Italian seasoning, cornstarch, dash of salt and black pepper. Stir well to mix. In a separate bowl, add the buttermilk.

Toss the chicken in the flour mix until coated on all sides. Dip into the buttermilk and roll again in the flour mix.

Drop the chicken into the hot oil. Fry for 5 minutes or until golden. Remove and transfer onto a plate lined with paper towels.

Serve the chicken with the waffles and a drizzle of hot sauce.

Smoked Salmon Breakfast Crackers

Smoked salmon is a much-enjoyed brunch item in several American cafes. Try it with this sweet and creamy avocado spread and you'll be a convert, too.

Servings: 2-4 servings

Total Time: 5 mins

Ingredients:

- 1 medium ripe avocado
- 4 ounces cream cheese
- 1 tbsp. honey
- 1 tsp. grated orange zest
- Pinch of sea salt
- 8 rye crackers or crispbreads
- 4 to 6 ounces smoked salmon
- 1 tbsp. chopped chives

Directions:

In a bowl, mash avocado using a fork. Add in the cream cheese, honey, orange zest and salt and stir with a spoon until well combined.

Spread the avocado mixture on the crackers, and top with smoked salmon and chives.

Enjoy!

Apricot Ricotta Bagels

These delicious bagels are the perfect lazy-day breakfast option. This recipe is good with other stone fruits like peaches, nectarines, or plums.

Servings: 2 servings

Total Time: 5-10 mins

Ingredients:

- 1 cup low-fat ricotta cheese
- 1 tbsp. honey
- 1/2 tsp. ground cinnamon
- 1/2 tsp. vanilla extract
- 2 bagels of choice, sliced in half
- 4 fresh apricots, thinly sliced
- 1/4 cup coarsely chopped pistachios

Directions:

Combine the ricotta, honey, cinnamon and vanilla. Toast the bagel halves.

Spread the cheese mixture on the toasted bagels, and top with apricot slices and pistachios.

Enjoy!

Kale Slaw With Hazelnut Dressing

Nobody loves Kale the way Americans do! This is a delicious combination of kale, kohlrabi, hazelnuts and fruit is rich, buttery, sweet and fresh.

Makes: 6 servings

Prep: 15-20 mins

Ingredients:

- 1 medium kohlrabi, peeled and shredded (about 1 cup)
- 1/4 tsp. plus 1/8 tsp. sea salt, divided
- 6 cups kale (about 1/2 bunch)
- 1/3 cup whole hazelnuts
- 2 tbsp. cider vinegar
- 1 tsp. grated orange zest
- 1 tsp. grainy mustard
- 2 tsp. fresh thyme
- 1 clove garlic, minced

- 1/4 tsp. freshly ground black pepper
- 1/3 cup extra virgin olive oil
- 1 large of red or orange bell pepper, thinly sliced
- 2 medium carrots, peeled and shredded
- 2 medium apples or pears, thinly sliced
- 1/3 cup dried cranberries or cherries
- Parmesan cheese, shaved (optional)

Directions:

Place the kohlrabi in a small bowl, toss with 1/8 tsp. of the salt and let sit 10 minutes. Drain as much water as possible and set aside.

Fold each leaf of kale in half lengthwise and slice out the center rib. Discard the ribs. Roll a stack of the leaves and slice in half lengthwise, then crosswise into very ¬ne ribbons. Add to a large bowl.

Place the hazelnuts, cider vinegar, orange zest, mustard, thyme, garlic, remaining 1/4 tsp. olive oil, salt and pepper in a food processor or blender container, and blend until well combined but still slightly chunky.

Toss together the kale and hazelnut dressing. With clean hands, firmly massage the greens for about 1 minute, or until tender. Add the kohlrabi, bell pepper, carrot, apple or pear, and dried cranberries or cherries to the kale, and toss to mix. Place on serving plates and garnish with shaved Parmesan if desired.

Enjoy!

Grilled Fruit Skewers

For sweet and savory sensation, red onion wedges are a nice addition to these skewers as well. Serve with grilled meats or seafood.

Total Time: 20m

Servings: 8

Ingredients:

- 1 firm, ripe mango, peeled and cut from the pit into chunks
- 1 firm, ripe papaya, peeled, seeded, cut into chunks
- 1 firm, ripe banana, peeled, cut into chunks
- ½ pineapple, peeled, cored, cut into chunks
- Grated zest and juice of 4 limes
- 2 tbsp. brown sugar
- A few drops of chili oil Salt

Directions:

Soak 24 bamboo skewers in water about 30 minutes.

Thread a piece of each type of fruit onto each skewer. Set aside.

Combine the lime zest and juice, brown sugar, and chili oil in a small bowl and whisk until the sugar is dissolved. Pour over the fruit and let stand for 15 to 30 minutes.

Preheat a grill or broiler. Sprinkle the fruit lightly with salt and grill, basting with the marinade and turning frequently, until lightly browned, 3 to 5 minutes. Serve with a little drizzle of the marinade.

Sriracha And Cheddar Burgers

Pin these burgers with stacked gooey cheeses in between two sriracha-seasoned beef patties to be on your next -to do lists. The burgers are very simple to do by placing the burgers on toasted hamburger buns and top with fried eggs if you desire.

Total Time: 1h 10m

Ingredients:

- 1 pound ground beef
- 1 tbsp. sriracha
- 1 tsp. Worcestershire sauce
- Salt
- Pepper
- 1/4 cup chopped fresh cilantro
- 2 tsp. garlic powder
- 4 slices cheddar cheese
- 1 tbsp. butter
- Fried eggs (optional)

- 2 toasted hamburger buns

Directions:

1. Combine the ground beef, sriracha, Worcestershire sauce, garlic powder, cilantro, salt and pepper. Mix with your hands until fully combined.

2. Shape into four balls and mold into a large patty, larger than a cheese slice.

3. Break into four pieces each cheese slice. Place two piles with a total of 8 cheese pieces, and stack in the middle of beef patty Cover the cheese with another patty, and tightly seal the edges by pinching together to keep the cheese intact during cooking. Repeat this process with the second burger.

4. Heat the butter in a large pan to moderate heat and cook the burgers for four minutes per side.

5. When done, place the burgers on the toasted hamburger buns. Top with fried egg if desired.

6. Serve!

Mini Macs

Go crazy with these unlimited Mini Macs, your own version of McDonald's big Mac! These fun sized burgers are the perfect appetizers for picky eaters or simply for a small gathering!

Total Time: 1h 5m

Servings: 6

Ingredients:

Special sauce:

- 1/4 tsp. salt
- 3 tbsp. yellow mustard
- 3/4 cup mayonnaise
- 1 tsp. white vinegar
- 1 tbsp. relish
- 1 tsp. of onion powder
- 1 tsp. of garlic powder
- 1/4 tsp. paprika

Burgers:

- 1/2 tsp. garlic powder
- 1/2 cup plain breadcrumbs
- 2 pounds ground beef
- 1/8 tsp. salt
- 1 medium finely diced onion
- 9 slices American cheese
- 12 dill pickle slices
- 1 package shredded iceberg lettuce
- Sesame seed buns:
- 2 tbsp. melted butter
- 12 slider rolls
- 1 tbsp. sesame seeds

Directions:

Preheat the oven at 425 degrees Fahrenheit.

Sauce: Whisk all special sauce ingredients until combined thoroughly, set aside.

Burgers: Combine in a large bowl with the ground beef, garlic powder, breadcrumbs, pepper and salt.

Drop six spoonfuls of beef mixture on a large greased rimmed baking sheet and gently press to form an even layer of patties.

Bake the patties for thirteen to fifteen minutes until no longer pink. Drain excess oil and top with cheese slices. Bake for 1 minute longer until the cheese melts.

For the buns:

Slice the entire slider rolls into three sheets and brush the top part with melted butter. Sprinkle with sesame seeds.

Brush the half layer with butter and place all slider buns on the baking sheet. Broil for thirty seconds until lightly toasted.

Brush with the special sauce along the bun bottoms and place on top with lettuce and onion.

Place on top a layer of burger patties and top with the bun middle section. Repeat the same layer procedure and add pickles on top and followed by sesame seed buns.

Using a chef's knife, score the buns and separate into six burgers.

Enjoy!

Cheesy Jalapeno Pretzel Bites

Fluffy, cheesy, and gooey, these jalapeno pretzel bites are easy and delicious at the same time!

Total Time: 2h 40m

Servings: 12

Ingredients:

- 1 package active dry yeast
- 1 cup warm water
- 1 tbsp. brown sugar
- 3 ¼ cups bread flour
- ½ cup cold beer
- 2 tbsp. unsalted butter, cubed, at room temperature, plus more for greasing
- 2 tsp salt
- 2 cups grated cheddar
- 2 jalapeno peppers, sliced thinly
- Coarse salt for topping

Directions:

Preheat oven to 500 F.

Add warm water to the bowl of a mixer. Sprinkle on the yeast

Add in the brown sugar. Mix thoroughly and allow to bloom until foamy. This should take about 5 minutes.

Add in the flour, butter, salt, and beer, and continue stirring. On low speed, begin kneading the dough for a minute or until it forms a smooth ball. Continue kneading until the dough become pliant about 5 minutes.

In a lightly greased bowl, place dough and cover with saran wrap. Allow to rise in a warm place for 90 minutes, until double.

Place dough onto a floured surface and divide into 12 equal portions.

Roll each piece out into a rectangle. Place a bit of cheese in the center (about 2 tbsp.) and top with a 3-4 jalapeno slices.

Pull the two edges of the dough together and pinch to cover. Ensure the cheese is completely covered and set onto a baking tray.

Do this with the rest of the cheese and dough. Place dough pieces 2 inches apart.

Allow to rise for 30 more minutes.

Coat with a quick egg wash before baking for 8-10 minutes until crispy and golden brown!

Top with coarse salt before serving!

Boneless Buffalo Wings

Tangy, crispy, and straight up delicious buffalo wings are a delicious appetizer for a fun weekend party! And a classic American bar food.

Total Time: 45m

Servings: 4

Ingredients:

Chicken

- 1 cup flour
- ¼ cup corn starch
- 1 1/2 tsp. ground black pepper
- 2 tsp. paprika
- 2 tsp. salt
- 1/2 tsp. cayenne powder
- 1/2 tsp. garlic powder
- 4 skinless, boneless chicken breasts, bite sized pieces
- 1 egg

- 1 cup milk

Buffalo Sauce

- 1 cup hot sauce
- 1/3 cup thick cream
- 1 tbsp. butter

Directions:

To make the sauce, combine all ingredients in a saucepan and cook until it starts boiling. Allow to cook until slightly thickened. Remove from heat and set aside.

In a large bowl, combine all the dry ingredients. In a separate bowl, mix egg and milk together. Begin coating the chicken dry wet dry and set on a tray.

In a large frying pan, heat oil on medium heat and fry the chicken pieces until cooked through and golden.

Transfer to a paper towel-lined baking sheet.

Place chicken in a flat serving tray and drizzle with buffalo sauce until coated.

Serve immediately!

Grilled Cheese Burger

These cheesy grilled burgers are simple to prepare, yet the taste is mega-delicious. It is the cheddar and butter that bring extra flavor to the sandwiches that are placed on the top and bottom of the grilled beef patty, since this recipe does not call any other ingredients to enhance the flavor. An American favourite!

Total Time: 1h 10m

Servings: 2

Ingredients:

- 4 tbsp. butter
- 8 white bread slices
- 8 cheddar slices
- 3/4 pounds ground beef
- Freshly ground black pepper
- Kosher salt

For serving:

- Ketchup

Directions:

Spread a tbsp. of butter onto 1 side of each slice. Top each butter-free bread slice with two cheddar slices. Place another bread slice on top with the butter side facing up.

Heat up a large nonstick pan on moderate heat and place the sandwiches in batches.

Cook each side until lightly golden brown and the cheeses have melted.

Remove sandwiches and wipe the skillet clean.

Prepare the burger by adding salt and pepper and cook in the same skillet over medium-high heat until each side is seared for four minutes. Remove burger patty from pan.

To assemble, place the grilled cheese on a large plate. Top the cheese with burger and then top with another grilled cheese and cut into half.

Serve burger with ketchup.

Enjoy!

Blue Cheese Burgers

Nightcap would be more enjoyable by serving these cheesy burgers with lettuce and caramelized onions with crispy rosemary.

Total Time: 1h

Servings: 4

Ingredients:

- 3 tbsp. olive oil
- 1 tsp. kosher salt, divided
- 2 medium onions, thinly sliced
- 4 fresh rosemary sprigs
- 4 ounces blue cheese
- 1/2 tsp. ground black pepper
- 1 1/2 pounds ground chuck
- 4 burger buns
- 8 lettuce leaves

Directions:

Heat oil in a large pan on moderate heat and cook the rosemary for 1 minute until crisp-tender.

Remove the sprigs with tongs and drain. Pull the rosemary leaves from its sprigs.

Cook the onions in the same skillet and season with ¼ tsp. of salt, stirring to coat well. Cook, covered, for 7 to 8 mins more until softened. Uncover and cook for additional 7 to 8 minutes until caramelized and soft.

Remove onions from heat and add the rosemary, stir to combine

Preheat the oven at 400 degrees F and position the oven rack in the center.

Shape ground beef into four equal-sized patties, with 3/4 –inch thickness.

Season each side with dash of pepper and ¾ tsp. salt.

Heat a cast-iron skillet on medium heat and cook the patties for five to six minutes until the bottom produced a nice brown crust.

Turn the patties, cook for five to six minutes for medium doneness; transfer to a sheet pan.

Crumble blue cheese evenly on top of each burger and bake for two to three minutes until melty.

Assemble the burger in this order: buns, burger patties, lettuce, and caramelized onions with rosemary.

Serve!

Dark Chocolate Brownies

Fudgy, moist and intensely chocolatey with a crackling top, these brownies are super easy to make and a dream to eat.

Makes: 16 brownies

Prep: 15 mins

Cook: 25 mins

Ingredients:

- 1 cup icing sugar
- 1 stick unsalted butter
- 3 eggs
- 1 cup all-purpose flour
- ½ cup + 2 tbsp. cocoa powder
- 3 oz. dark chocolate, chopped

Directions:

Preheat the oven to 375°F. Prepare an 8x8 inch baking tin.

In a large pan on low, combine butter and sugar until all the butter has melted.

Remove the pan from the heat. Add in the flour, eggs, and cocoa. Lastly, fold in the dark chocolate.

Pour batter into the tin. Place in oven for about twenty five minutes or until the edges are set and the top looks firm.

Let the brownies cool before cutting.

Lemon Tart

Sweet, zesty and light, this tart is the perfect after-dessert treat.

Makes: 8 servings

Prep: 2 hrs. 10 mins

Cook: 30 mins

Ingredients:

For the pastry:

- 1 ¾ cup all-purpose flour
- 4 tbsp. icing sugar
- ½ tsp salt
- ¼ cup unsweetened cocoa powder
- ½ cup unsalted butter
- 1 egg yolk
- 2 ½ tbsp. cold water

For the tart:

- ½ cup dark chocolate, grated finely
- 2 large lemons
- 2/3 cup caster sugar
- 4 eggs
- ½ cup + 2 tbsp. heavy cream
- Icing sugar, for dusting

Directions:

For the pastry:

In a bowl, combine together the salt, cocoa, sugar, and flour. Add the butter and mix. Add the egg yolk and then the water. Mix well. Fold into a lump. Wrap with cling film and chill for 40 minutes.

Roll out the pastry evenly onto the base of a well-greased 9-inch spring form cake tin and chill for 90 minutes.

For the tart:

Preheat oven to 400°F. Place in the oven for 15 minutes. Do not overbake. Immediately sprinkle the hot pastry evenly with the grated chocolate. Set aside. Reduce oven temperature to 325°F.

Grate the zest into a bowl. Add the sugar and the juice from the lemons. Mix well. Whisk in the eggs and then the cream until well incorporated. Pour over the pastry in the spring form tin and bake for about 30 minutes or until set.

Release the spring form-tin sides to aid cooling. Allow to cool completely. Dust with sugar and serve.

White Chocolate Muffins

Enjoy these soft, moist and wonderfully rich white chocolate muffins for breakfast or dessert!

Makes: 6 muffins

Prep: 10 mins

Cook: 20 mins

Ingredients:

- 1 cup + 2 tbsp. all-purpose flour
- 1 tsp. vanilla extract
- 1 ½ tsp. baking powder
- 6 tbsp. white sugar
- ¼ tsp. salt
- 1 small egg or ½ a large egg

- ½ cup buttermilk
- 4 tbsp. vegetable oil
- ½ cup white chocolate, chopped

Directions:

Preheat the oven to 425°F. Line a muffin pan with 6 liners.

Combine dry ingredients in a different bowl.

Beat together the egg, buttermilk, oil and vanilla extract until well combined. Add in the flour and sugar mixture and stir until just combined. Fold in the white chocolate.

Divide batter evenly between the cupcake liners. Bake for about 5 minutes then lower the heat to 350°F and bake for 15 minutes more.

Place on a cooling rack to cool.

Enjoy!

Basic Buttermilk Waffles

Classic American breakfast - this recipe the base for your own waffle creations. You can fold in pretty much anything into this batter and you can serve these yummy waffles topped with any fruit or sugary sauce you like.

Total Time: 20m

Servings: 4

Ingredients:

- 1 ¾ cup Buttermilk
- 3 tsp Vanilla
- 4 tsp Baking Powder
- 2 cups Flour
- 3 tbsp. Sugar
- ½ cup Butter, melted
- 2 Eggs

Ingredients:

1. Preheat your waffle iron to high.

2. Combine the dry ingredients in a bowl.

3. Whisk together the wet ones in another.

4. Gently combine the two mixtures.

5. Spoon some of the batter into your waffle iron.

6. Cook for about 5 minutes, or until golden.

7. Repeat with the remaining batter.

8. Serve with your favorite toppings and enjoy!

Pecan Pie

No American recipe book would be complete without the addition of a classic pecan pie recipe.

Makes: 12-16 slices

Prep: 1 ½ hrs.

Cook: 1 hr.

Ingredients:

Pie Dough:

- ¾ cup all-purpose flour, sifted
- ½ tsp. salt
- 4 ½ tbsp. cold unsalted butter, cubed
- 2 tbsp. ice water

Filling:

- 4 eggs
- 1 cup light corn syrup

- 1/3 cup packed light brown sugar
- ¼ cup granulated sugar
- ¼ cup unsalted butter, melted
- 1 tsp. sea salt
- 3 cups pecan halves
- 1 tsp. vanilla extract

For serving:

- Vanilla ice cream or whipped cream

Directions:

Process the flour & salt in a food processor and pulse to combine.

Add the unsalted butter and pulse until the butter is broken up into lumps about the size of small peas.

Add the water, 1/2 tbsp. at a time, pulsing as you go, until the mixture has a barely sticky, dough like texture.

Move mixture to a bowl and then gently work the dough with your hands until it forms a firm ball. Shape it into a disk, cover it in plastic wrap, and chill in the refrigerator for at least 1 hour.

Preheat the oven to 375°F.

Remove the dough and let sit at on the counter for 5 minutes. On a floured surface, roll out the dough into a circle of about 13 inches. in diameter.

Gently fold the circle in 1/2, & then in half again, so it looks like a quarter wedge of a circle. Center the point of the wedge in a 10-inch pie plate and gently unfold the dough.

Trim the dough so that just 1 inch hangs over the sides. Fold the overhanging dough under itself to form a rim. Crimp this rim between your thumb and forefinger to form a patterned edge around the edges of the pie plate.

Bake the crust for 5 minutes. Remove and set it aside. This is not prebaking the crust but giving it a bit of a head start for a very wet pie filling.

Lower the oven temperature to 350 degrees. For the filling, combine the 4 eggs, corn syrup, sugars, butter, salt, and vanilla in a large bowl. Whisk until smooth. Stir in the pecans.

Pour the mixture into the pie crust.

Bake for an hour, or until the filling jiggles just slightly in the center when gently shaken.

Let the pie cool completely, approximately 2 hours, before serving. Serve with vanilla ice cream or whipped cream.

Triple Chocolate Cookies

Get thrice the amount of chocolate in one bite with these soft, chewy and insanely addicting triple chocolate chip cookie recipe!

Makes: 9 servings

Prep: 30 mins

Cook: 10 mins

Ingredients:

- 4 tbsp. unsalted butter, room temperature
- 6 tbsp. white sugar
- 2 tbsp. brown sugar
- 1 small egg
- ½ + 1/8 tsp. vanilla extract
- ½ cup all-purpose flour
- ¼ tsp. salt
- ¼ + 1/8 tsp. baking powder
- 3 tbsp. unsweetened cocoa powder
- ¼ + 1/8 tsp. baking soda

- ¼ cup milk chocolate chips
- ¼ cup dark chocolate chips

Directions:

Beat butter and sugars for 3 minutes. Add in the egg, vanilla extract and milk beat until well combined.

Combine dry ingredients in a different bowl.

Working in batches of three, add the dry mixture to the butter mixture and beat until just combined. Fold in the dark chocolate chips. Cover and refrigerate for 20 minutes.

Preheat the oven to 350°F. Line and grease a baking pan with baking paper.

Scoop out 2 tbsp. of dough for each cookie and place on pan, leaving a 2 inch gap between each ball. Bake for 8-14 minutes or until the edges of the cookies are crisp.

Place on a cooling rack to cool completely.

Enjoy!

White Chocolate Blueberry Tart

Blueberry and white chocolate tart with a chocolate shortbread pastry crust.

Makes: 4 servings

Prep: 20 mins

Cook: 20 mins

Ingredients:

For the chocolate shortbread pastry:

- 1 ¼ cups all-purpose flour
- 3/8 cup unsalted butter
- Generous 3/8 cup white sugar
- 2 egg yolks
- 1/4 tsp baking powder
- 7 tsp cocoa powder
- Vanilla powder
- Salt

For the Filling:

41

- Generous 3/8 cup cream
- 2 tsp glucose syrup
- 7 oz. white chocolate
- 3 oz. blueberry jam

For the decoration:

- 9 oz. fresh blueberries
- Confectioners' (icing) sugar

Directions:

Prepare the shortbread pastry: Mix the softened butter with the sugar, stir in a pinch of salt and the egg. Add the flour, baking powder, cocoa and a pinch of vanilla powder, then knead briefly until you have a smooth, even paste.

Plastic wrap the dough and refrigerate for one hour. On a lightly floured surface, roll out 9 oz. of the shortbread pastry to a thickness of 1/8 in (3 mm).

Line a buttered, floured cake tin with the pastry. Spread with blueberry jam and bake at 350 °F (180 °C) for 18 to 20 minutes. Remove and cool, then remove the tart from the tin.

Chop the white chocolate and put it in a bowl. Boil the cream with the syrup and pour it over the chocolate. Mix well until you have smooth, velvety cream.

Leave to cool and pour into the tart shell until it is filled up to the brim. Garnish with fresh blueberries, which have been washed and dried. Sprinkle with confectioners' sugar before serving.

White Chocolate Blondies

Take a break from regular brownies and enjoy these gooey, moist and absolutely delicious white chocolate blondies.

Makes: 12 servings

Prep: 5 mins

Cook: 30 mins

Ingredients:

- 2 sticks unsalted butter
- 4 large eggs
- 1 1/2 cups white sugar
- ½ cup brown sugar
- 1 tsp. vanilla extract
- 2 cups all-purpose flour
- 1 tsp. salt
- 1 1/4 cups white chocolate chips
- Vanilla ice cream, for serving

Directions:

Preheat the oven to 325°F. Line a 9x13 inch baking pan with baking paper and set aside.

In a medium-sized bowl, melt together the butter and white chocolate chips in a microwave in 20 second intervals. Set aside to cool.

Beat together the eggs, white sugar, brown sugar and vanilla extract until well combined. Add in the butter mixture followed by the flour and salt and beat again until just combined.

Pour into the pan and bake for about half an hour.

Serve with vanilla ice cream and enjoy!

Grilled Wings + Sauce

We bake and fry chicken wings but there is nothing like grilled wings. You grill them super fast and are delicious and crispy. Plus, the sauce gives additional satisfaction. Perfect for a traditional American BBQ day.

Prep: 10min

Cook: 15min

Total Time: 25min

Servings: 4

Ingredients:

- 1 Lemon, the zest
- 2 tsp. Salt
- ¼ tsp. Cayenne
- 1 tsp. Thyme, dried
- 1 tsp. of Onion powder
- 1 tsp. of Garlic powder
- 1 tsp. of Smoked Paprika

- Oil
- 2 lb. Wings

Sauce:

- 1 tbsp. Mustard
- 1 Lemon, the juice
- ½ cup of Mayo
- 2 tsp. Chives, chopped, fresh
- 2 tsp. of Horseradish
- 1 tsp. of Hot sauce

Directions:

1. In a bowl combine the cayenne, thyme, onion powder, garlic powder, paprika, salt, and lemon zest. Stir to combine. Coat the wings with the spice mixture.

2. Turn on the grill to medium. Oil the grates and place the wings. Cook for 20 minutes.

3. In the meantime cake the sauce. In a bowl combine the hot sauce, chives, horseradish, mustard, lemon juice, and mayo.

4. Once the wings are done serve hot with the sauce on the side.

5. Enjoy!

Basic Soft Pretzels

This is a quick and easy pretzel recipe, perfect for evening snack or a late night delight!

Total Time: 2h 20m

Servings: 8

Ingredients:

- 1 package active dry yeast
- 1 cup warm water
- 1 tbsp. brown sugar
- 3 ¼ cups bread flour
- ½ cup cold beer
- 2 tbsp. unsalted butter, cut into 1 inch pieces, at room temperature, plus more for greasing
- 2 tsp salt

Ingredients:

Preheat oven to 500 F.

Into a stand mixer, add in the warm water. Sprinkle on the yeast

Add in the brown sugar. Mix thoroughly and allow to bloom until foamy. This should take about 5 minutes.

Add in the flour, butter, salt, and beer, and continue stirring. On low speed, begin kneading the dough for a minute or until it forms a smooth ball. Continue kneading until the dough become pliant about 5 minutes.

In a lightly greased bowl, place dough and cover with saran wrap. Set away to rise in a warm area for 90 minutes, until double.

Divide into 8 portions and roll into desired shape knots, buns, or sticks.

Arrange on 2 lined baking trays about 2 inches apart.

Allow to rise for 30 more minutes.

Coat with a quick egg wash before baking for 8-10 minutes until crispy and golden brown!

Ribs

Don't try to cut the fat off because it will melt and flavor the meat as well as help it cook. Ribs are a local favourite and every American diner has its own version!

Prep time: 5 minutes

Cooking time: 10 minutes

Serves: 2

Ingredients:

- 4 tsp. chili powder
- 1/2 tsp. cayenne pepper
- 2 tsp. table salt
- 1 1/2 tsp. pepper
- 3–4 beef rib slabs (5 pounds total)

Preparation:

Put two large chunks of wood in water for an hour.

Mix the spices in a bowl and rub them on the ribs then let stand for one hour.

Light about 30 charcoal briquettes and after about ten minutes put the coals to one side and add a piece of wood partially on the coals.

Put the meat, meat side down, over the cool side (where the wood is). Close the vents to two-thirds and leave for about an hour. The temperature should be about 300 F and 250 F after the first hour.

After the first hour has passed, add 20 more briquettes and the other chunk of wood and flip the meat and rotate so the part that was farthest from the coals is now closest.

It should be ready in about 90 minutes.

Serve with barbeque sauce.

Nyc Street Hotdogs

These delicious hotdogs are an NYC staple and once you try this recipe, you'll understand why!

Serving Size: 6 servings

Total Time: 40m

Ingredients:

- 6 hotdogs
- 6 hot dog buns

For Onion relish.

- 2 tbsp. oil
- 3 yellow onions, sliced
- 3 cloves garlic, minced
- 1/3 cup marinara or tomato sauce
- 1/2 cup mL water
- 2 tbsp. paprika
- 1 tsp. brown sugar
- 1/2 tsp. cayenne
- 1/2 tsp. salt

- 1/2 tsp. black pepper

Ingredients:

To prepare the sauce, heat oil and add in the onions. Cook for 3-5 minutes.

Add garlic and cook for 2 additional mins.

Add in the tomato sauce, water, paprika, brown sugar and cayenne. Allow to simmer for 15-20 minutes.

Season with salt and pepper.

While sauce is simmering, preheat your grill on medium heat. Cook hotdogs for 6-8 minutes, turning occasionally.

Once cooked through, place into warmed buns.

Top with onion relish and serve!

Candy Apple | Enchanted

These candy apples are a fun party food and an instant hit with the kids! A classic American fair food!

Serving Size: 8 servings

Total Time: 1hr

Ingredients:

- 8 small crisp apples, washed and dried, with stems removed
- Ice-cream sticks
- 2 cups sugar
- 1/2 tsp. vinegar1/2 cup water
- 1/2 tsp. red food coloring (optional)

Ingredients:

Using baking paper, line a tray and set aside.

Insert an ice-cream stick into the top of each apple.

In a deep set sauce pan, add the sugar and vinegar and bring the mixture to a boil.

Use a wet pastry brush to brush down on any sugar that sticks to the sides. This prevents burning. DO NOT stir the mixture.

Once it boils bring to a simmer for 20 minutes. Swirl the mixture slightly, evenly melting the sugar. Use a candy thermometer if you've got one and check for the mixture to read 300 F which is the hard crack stage.

To test without a thermometer, drop a small tsp. of the sugar mixture into cold water. If the sugar becomes hard instantly and cracks when tapped on, it is ready to use.

You can add in the food coloring at this stage if using. Swirl to color evenly.

Remove from heat and allow the bubbles to dissipate.

To cover the apples, carefully tilt the pan to one side and holding onto the ice-cream stick, dip the apple into the sugar mixture, rotating till covered completely.

Wait for it to stop dripping too much and place the apple onto the baking paper to cool and harden.

Corn Dogs | Princess Diaries

If you've been to a classic America adventure park, you've probably eaten a corndog! These corndogs are crispy in the best kind of way!

Serving Size: 8 servings

Total Time: 30m

Ingredients:

- 1 cup all-purpose flour
- 1 1/4 cups cornmeal
- 3 Tbsp. sugar
- 1/4 tsp. salt
- 2.5 tsp. baking powder
- 1 egg
- 1 1/4 cups buttermilk
- 1 tbsp. vegetable oil
- 2.5 tsp. honey
- 8 hotdogs
- Wooden skewers
- Vegetable Oil, for frying

Ingredients:

In a deep set pan, heat oil on medium.

In a mixing bowl, combine the flour, sugar, cornmeal, baking powder, and salt. Add in the egg, buttermilk, honey and oil. Mix until combined.

Remove hotdogs from package and wipe dry.

Insert a wooden skewer into each hotdog.

Hold each skewer and dip into prepared batter. This is easiest if you pour the batter into a narrow container or a large glass. Make sure to coat the entire hotdog.

Remove from batter, allowing excess to drip off. Holding onto the skewer, move it to the hot oil. Hold and cook for 2-3 minutes until hotdog is evenly golden brown.

Remove from oil and set on paper towels to absorb excess oil. Repeat with the rest of the hotdogs.

Serve with your favorite dips!

Nyc Pizza

If you've been to New York City, you'll notice they are a little passionate about their pizza. You'll see why!

Serving Size: 2 13-inch pizzas

Total Time: 2hr

Ingredients:

Pizza Dough

- 3 1/2 - 4 cups bread flour (can be substituted with all-purpose flour)
- 2 ¼ tsp. instant dry yeast
- 1 tsp. sugar
- 2 tsp. salt
- 2 tbsp. olive oil
- 1 ½ cups water, 110 degrees F

Pizza Sauce

- 2 (8 oz.) cans tomato sauce

- 1/4 cup tomato paste
- 1 1/2 tbsp. extra virgin olive oil
- 1 1/2 tsp. honey
- 2 tsp. chopped fresh oregano
- 2 tsp. chopped fresh basil
- 1/4 tsp. dried thyme (or 3/4 tsp. fresh)
- 1 clove garlic, finely minced
- Salt and pepper, to taste

Topping

40 slices pepperoni

½ cup finely shredded parmesan cheese

4 cups shredded mozzarella cheese

2 tbsp. fresh oregano chopped.

Ingredients:

In the bowl of a stand mixer, or a large bowl if using a handheld mixer, combine the flour, yeast, sugar, and salt.

With the mixer on slow, drizzle in the oil and water, mixing until the dough comes together.

Should the dough be very sticky, you can add in a little more flour. If it is too dry, add in a tbsp. more of water.

Once it comes together, begin kneading on a floured surface until the dough is smooth and firm.

Place dough into a large bowl greased with olive oil. Cover with plastic wrap and leave to rise for 1 hour. You want to leave the bowl in a warm place.

Once risen, divide the dough into 2 and cover with a clean towel to rest for another 10 minutes.

As the dough rests, prepare the sauce by combining all the ingredients together and allowing to develop for 40 minutes. This is optional, you may always use store bought pizza sauce.

Preheat oven to 450 F.

On a floured surface, begin rolling out the pizza dough into a 13 inch round shape.

Spread pizza sauce over dough and layer pepperoni slices on top. Add veggies if desired and finally sprinkle on the cheese!

Bake for 12-15 minutes or until browned.

Remove from oven and sprinkle with oregano. Enjoy your real pizza!

Hot Chocolate

Hot Chocolate is basically a divine creation come fall time and an absolutely delicious staple!

Serving Size: 2 servings

Total Time: 15m

Ingredients:

- 2 cups whole milk
- 2 tbsp. sugar
- 4 oz. bittersweet chocolate chopped (scant 1 cup)
- ¼ tsp vanilla extract
- Whipped cream and marshmallows (optional)

Ingredients:

Mix milk and sugar in a small saucepan and set on the stovetop over medium heat.

In the meantime, put the chocolate into a bowl and microwave in 20 second intervals, stirring each time, until just melted.

When bubbles start to appear on the surface of the milk, turn off the heat and add in the melted chocolate. Whisk thoroughly to combine.

Add the vanilla extract and pour into serving mugs.

Top with marshmallows and whipped cream if needed!

Hawaiian Punch

Hawaiian Punch is a delicious way to beat the heat in the hotter months!

Serving Size: 10 servings

Total Time: 4hr

Ingredients:

Juice

- 1 (6-ounce) can orange juice, thawed
- 1 (6-ounce) can lemonade, thawed
- 1 (24-ounce) can pineapple juice

Sugar Syrup

- 1 ½ cups water
- 1 ½ cups sugar
- ½ lbs. strawberries.
- 2 cups lemon soda (recommended: Sprite)

Ingredients:

In a large bowl, combine the different juices and stir well.

Leave to chill in the freezer while you make the sugar syrup.

Hull the strawberries and place them into the freezer.

Prepare the sugar syrup by combing the sugar and water in a saucepan. Heat on medium heat and bring to a boil. Keep cooking until all the sugar has completely dissolved. Remove from heat.

Allow it to cool completely. Once cooled, mix in with the juice mixture.

Refrigerate for half an hour.

To serve, pour the fruit juice into a large jug or punch bowl. Add in the soda and stir. Finally, add in the frozen strawberries and serve!

Shrimp Tacos With Tomatillo Black Bean Salsa

Tacos are an American favourite! The tart, apple-flavored flesh of the tomatillo punches up the light and refreshing salsa in this recipe.

Makes: 4 servings

Prep: 10 mins

Ingredients:

For the salsa:

- 2 cups diced tomatillo
- 1 cup cubed pineapple
- 1 cup canned black beans, rinsed and drained
- 1/2 small red onion, finely diced
- 1 jalapeño chile pepper, seeded and minced
- 2 cloves garlic, minced

- 1/2 cup chopped cilantro

Juice of 1 lime

- 1/2 tsp. ground cumin
- 1/4 tsp. sea salt

For the tacos:

- 1/2 pound frozen and thawed cooked shrimp
- 8 (6 to 8-inch) corn or whole wheat tortillas

Directions:

For the salsa: In a large bowl, toss together the tomatillo, pineapple, black beans, onion, chile pepper, garlic, cilantro, lime juice, cumin and salt.

For the tacos: Divide the shrimp among the tortillas and top with the salsa.

Enjoy!

Tex-Mex Chipotle Beans

A truly American creation tex mex! This fiber-packed dish makes for wonderful leftovers.

Makes: 6 servings

Prep: 10 mins

Ingredients:

- 1 (14-ounce) can each white navy beans, kidney beans and black beans, rinsed and drained
- 1 large red bell pepper, chopped
- 1 large avocado, diced
- 1 cup corn kernels, canned or frozen and thawed
- 1/4 cup hemp seeds (optional)
- 1 pound tomatoes (about 3 medium), quartered
- 1/2 small onion, finely diced
- 1/3 cup packed cilantro
- 1 tbsp. chopped chipotle chile pepper in adobo sauce
- 1 clove garlic, chopped

- 1 tsp. ground cumin
- Juice of 1/2 lime
- 1/4 tsp. sea salt
- 1/4 tsp. freshly ground black pepper
- 1/2 cup sour cream
- 1 cup sharp cheddar cheese or pepper Jack cheese, grated
- 1 cup coarsely crushed tortilla chips

Directions:

In a large bowl, toss together the beans, bell pepper, avocado, corn and hemp seeds, if using.

Add the tomato, onion, cilantro, chipotle chile pepper, lime juice, garlic, cumin, salt, and black pepper to a blender or food processor container and pulse until well combined but still slightly chunky.

Pulse in the sour cream.

Pour the tomato mix over the beans. Stir to coat. Stir in the cheese and tortilla chips. Serve at room temperature or chilled.

Enjoy!

Conclusion

There you go! 30 varied, delicious and easy American recipes for when you're craving your favorite American dish. Wings, Pizza, or Brownies? What are you most excited for? We've had a wonderful time writing this book for you and developing all the recipes you see.

We hope you enjoy this book and make sure to try out all the recipes and share them with your friends and family!

Part 2

Latin American Recipes

1. Mixed Squash Tacos

Ingredients:

- 1 avocado
- 1 cup coarsely grated Monterey Jack cheese
- 1 cup fresh corn kernels
- 1 lb mixed summer squash, sliced into ½ inch cube
- 1 tbsp adobo sauce more for garnish
- 1 tbsp extra-virgin olive oil
- ½ cup sour cream
- 8 6-inch flour tortillas
- Kosher salt
- Lime wedges, for garnish

Directions

- Add squash to skillet coated with heated oil, cook for about 4-5 minutes or until golden, spoon once.
- Spoon in 1 tsp salt, adobo sauce, corn kernels and cook for about 3-4 more minutes.
- Scatter mashed avocado onto tortillas.
- Add sour cream, cheese, squash mixture topping and splash adobo sauce (if desired)

- Serve alongside wedges.

2. Chipotle Chicken And Corn Tostadas

Ingredients:

- ½ cup coarsely chopped cilantro
- ½ cup sour cream
- ½ tsp dried oregano
- 1 chipotle in adobo sauce, minced + 2-½ Tbsp sauce
- 1 lb boneless, skinless chicken breast cutlets
- 1 tbsp canola or vegetable oil
- 2 tsp finely grated lime zest
- 2 tsp fresh lime juice
- 3 ears corn, husked
- 8 tostada shells
- Kosher salt
- Lime wedges, for serving (optional)

Directions

- Take a bowl; add ½ tsp salt, oregano, zest, oil, 2 tbsp adobo sauce, minced chipotle and toss to combine.
- Add chicken afterwards and toss to coat.
- Season corn with salt and brush lightly with oil.
- Prepare grill onto medium-high heat at 400 - 475 F.

- Grill corn as well as chicken for about 5-8 minutes and turn once after few minutes and charred for about 12 minutes.
- Arrange it to cutting board and chop corn and chicken in bite size pieces.
- Take a bowl; add ¼ tsp salt, ½ tbsp adobo sauce, lime juice as well as sour cream and combine.
- Scatter onto tostada shells. Add cilantro, chicken and corn topping.
- Serve alongside lime wedges.

3. Grilled Steak Skewers With Arugula Chimichuri

Ingredients:

- ½ cup olive oil
- ½ tsp dark brown sugar
- 1 lb sirloin steak, sliced in an inch cubes
- 1 medium red onion, sliced in an inch pieces
- 1 red bell pepper, sliced in an inch pieces
- 1 tsp smoked paprika
- ¼ tsp crushed red pepper flakes
- ¼ tsp ground cumin
- 10 oz cremini mushrooms, stemmed and wiped clean
- 2 medium cloves garlic, crushed
- 2 oz baby arugula
- 2 Tbsp red vinegar
- Freshly ground black pepper
- Kosher salt

Directions
- Prepare grill onto medium heat at 350 - 375 F.
- Take a bowl; add 1 tsp salt, cumin, brown sugar, paprika and combine.
- Add steak and toss to combine.

- Thread onion, mushrooms and steak in skewers one after the other.
- Grill for about 10 minutes or until steak is cooked or medium-rare.
- In the meantime, add ¼ tsp black pepper, 1 tsp salt, pepper flakes, vinegar, garlic, olive oil, arugula to food processor and process until smooth.
- Serve alongside skewers.

4. Seafood Guacamole

Ingredients:

- ¼ cup plus 2 Tbsp chopped fresh cilantro
- ½ tsp chipotle powder
- 1 ½ cup shredded fish
- 1 tbsp extra-virgin olive oil
- 2 6-7-oz ripe Hass avocados, preferably Mexican
- 2 Tbsp finely chopped white onion
- 2 Tbsp minced fresh serrano or jalapeño, including seeds
- 2 tsp fresh lime juice
- 3 Tbsp fresh orange juice
- Kosher salt

Directions
- Take a bowl; add ½ tsp salt, chipotle powder, olive oil, 1 tbsp chili, 2 tbsp cilantro, orange juice, fish and combine.
- Let it stand for about 25 minutes.
- Add ½ tsp salt, 1 tbsp chili, 2 tbsp cilantro, onion to a food processor and blend until paste.
- Halve avocados.
- Make crosshatch pattern in avocado flesh and scoop it to bowl.

- Combine lime juice, remaining cilantro alongside mashed avocado.
- Add 2/3 of it to seafood mixture.
- Season with chili, salt and more lime juice.
- Add guacamole topping alongside remaining seafood before you serve.

5. Grilled Chicken With Curried Couscous, Spinach And Mango

Ingredients:

- ¼ cup toasted slivered almonds
- 1 cup whole-wheat couscous
- 1 small firm-ripe mango, sliced in ½ inch dice
- 1 tbsp finely chopped fresh flat-leaf parsley
- 1 tbsp thinly sliced shallot
- 1 tsp curry powder
- 2 oz baby spinach
- 3 Tbsp white vinegar
- 4 boneless, skinless chicken breast halves
- 5 Tbsp + 1 tsp extra-virgin olive oil
- Kosher salt and freshly ground black pepper

Directions

- Prepare grill at 375 F.
- Add shallot to skillet coated with 1 tbsp heated olive oil and cook for about 2 minutes or until translucent.
- Add curry powder and cook for about 15 more seconds or until fragrant, spoon.
- Spoon in 3 tbsp olive oil as well as vinegar.

- Separate it from the heat and flavor with pepper as well as salt.
- Grill chicken (coated with pepper, ¼ tsp salt and 1 tbsp of olive oil) for about 12-15 minutes or until thoroughly cooked, flip once.
- Let it stand for a while before you transfer it to platter.
- In the meantime, boil ½ tsp salted water in a saucepan.
- Combine 1 tsp olive oil and couscous to coat.
- Add couscous to boiling water, cover and let it stand for about 6 minutes; spoon and fluff.
- Take a bowl; add parsley, almonds, mango, 3 tbsp vinaigrette and toss.
- Flavor with pepper and salt.
- Lightly coat spinach with vinaigrette.
- Distribute couscous among platters.
- Serve with topped chicken, spinach and splashed remaining vinaigrette.

6. Pernil-Style Beef Tenderloin

Ingredients:

- ½ tsp granulated sugar
- 1 1-¼-lb beef tenderloin
- 1 tbsp distilled white vinegar
- 1 tsp chili powder
- 2 small shallots, coarsely chopped
- 3 large cloves garlic, coarsely chopped
- ¾ tsp dried oregano
- ¾ tsp ground cumin
- 4 lime wedges
- 4 Tbsp extra-virgin olive oil
- Kosher salt and freshly ground black pepper

Directions

- Prepare oven at 400 F.
- Add ¼ tsp pepper, ¾ tsp salt, sugar, oregano, cumin, chili powder, vinegar, 3 tbsp oil, shallots, garlic to food processor and process until paste.
- Chop tenderloin in ½ inch slit.
- Scatter 1 tbsp on each slit and secure with wooden toothpicks.
- Flavor with pepper and salt.

- Add tenderloins to ovenproof skillet coated with 1 tbsp of heated oil and cook for about 4-5 minutes or until golden.
- Arrange skillet to oven and roast for about 10 minutes.
- Flip over and scatter remaining paste topping.
- Roast for about 7 minutes at 145 F.
- Arrange onto cutting board, remove toothpicks and let it stand for a while to cool.
- Chop in ½ inch pieces and serve alongside lime wedges.

7. Black Pepper Crusted Beef Tenderloin With Chimichurri Sauce

Ingredients:

For the chimichurri sauce

- ¼ tsp crushed red pepper flakes
- 1 tbsp chopped garlic
- 1 tbsp fresh oregano or 1 tsp dried
- 1 tbsp red vinegar
- 1 tsp fresh lime juice; more to taste
- 1/3 cup extra-virgin olive oil
- 1-½ oz mixed fresh cilantro and flat-leaf parsley leaves
- Kosher salt

For the steaks

- 1 tbsp olive oil
- 2 Tbsp black peppercorns, coarsely crushed
- 4 6-7-oz beef tenderloin steaks, about 1-½ inches thick
- Kosher or coarse salt

Directions

- Add garlic, oregano, parsley, cilantro to food processor and pulse until thinly sliced.
- Spoon in ½ tsp salt, red pepper flakes, lime juice, vinegar and olive oil to prepare sauce.
- Take a bowl; add 2 tsp salt as well as crushed peppercorns and combine.
- Coat both sides of the steak with mixture generously to coat.
- Keep it aside for about half an hour or 45 minutes.
- Prepare oven at 350 F.
- Add steaks to skillet coated with heated oil and cook for about 5 minutes onto medium-high heat or until browned.
- Flip and cook for 5 more minutes.
- Arrange skillet to oven and prepare for about 5-6 minutes or until medium-rare.
- Let it stand for a while, cover with foil and serve alongside chimichurri sauce topping.

8. Poblano And Ham Quesadillas

Ingredients:

- ½ lb mozzarella, grated
- 4 tsp unsalted butter
- 8 small flour tortillas
- 8 to 10 oz fresh poblanos, roasted, peeled, seeded, and sliced into ¼-inch strips
- 8 very thin slices Serrano ham, prosciutto, or other good cured ham

Directions

- Divide poblano strips, ham as well as cheese uniformly onto half of each tortilla.
- Fold and keep it aside.
- Add butter to skillet and heat until bubbles.
- Add folded tortillas to skillet and toast for about 3-4 minutes or until cheese melts.
- Flip halfway through.
- Do the same with remaining quesadillas before you serve.

9. Siloin Tacos

Ingredients:

- 1 tbsp kosher salt
- 1 tsp coarsely ground black pepper
- 1 tsp dried granulated garlic
- 1 tsp dried thyme
- 1 tsp Hungarian paprika
- 12-16 small flour or corn tortillas, warmed
- 2 lb sirloin steak, about an inch thick
- Roasted Tomato Salsa

Directions

- Add thyme, pepper, garlic, paprika, salt to a medium bowl and combine.
- Splash it onto steak and rub onto both sides.
- Let it stand for about 60 minutes on room temperature.
- Prepare the grill and coat with oil.
- Grill sirloin onto grate for about 4 minutes each side.
- Flip over and grill for 4 more minutes or until properly grilled.
- Arrange it in oven and prepare for about 4-6 minutes or until medium-rare.

- Chop steak on cutting board in diagonal strips and separate fats.
- Enjoy with roasted tomato salsa as well as warm tortilla.

10. Steak Adobo

Ingredients:

- ½ tsp finely ground black pepper
- 1 tbsp fresh lime juice
- 1 tbsp olive oil
- 1/8 tsp ground allspice
- 1/8 tsp ground cinnamon
- 2 tsp ancho chile powder
- 4 ½ inch-thick boneless rib-eye, New York strip
- Kosher salt

Directions

- Take a bowl; add all spice, cinnamon, pepper, chili powder and combine.
- Coat each side of steak with lime juice and generously flavor with salt.
- Splash all spices and let it stand for about 10 minutes.
- Add steaks to the skillet coated with heated oil and cook for about 2 minutes on medium-high heat; flip and continue cooking for about 2-3 more minutes or until medium rare.
- Repeat the process for remaining steak before you serve.

11. Chicken Fajitas With Red Pepper, Onion And Lime

Ingredients:

- 1 large red bell pepper, cored, seeded, and sliced into strips about ¼ inch wide and 2 inches long
- 1 tbsp fresh lime juice
- 1 very large or 2 medium yellow onions, quartered and thinly sliced crosswise
- 1-¼ tsp ground cumin
- 1-½ cups crumbled queso fresco or grated Monterey Jack cheese
- 1-½ tsp chili powder
- 2 Tbsp canola, vegetable, or corn oil
- 3 medium cloves garlic, minced
- 6-8 boneless, skinless chicken thighs, trimmed of excess fat
- Kosher salt and freshly ground black pepper
- 12 5-6-inch corn tortillas

Directions
- Take a bowl; add ½ tsp pepper, ¾ tsp salt, ½ tsp cumin, 1 tsp chili powder and combine.
- Rub spices on both sides of chicken.

- Add chicken to skillet coated with 1 tbsp of heated oil and cook for about 4-5 minutes onto medium-high heat or until golden.
- Separate it from the heat and arrange onto cutting board to chop.
- In the meantime, add ½ tsp pepper, ½ tsp salt, bell pepper, onion to another skillet coated with remaining 1 tbsp heated oil and cook for about 3-4 minutes onto medium-high heat or until fragrant, spoon often.
- Spoon in ½ tsp chili powder, ¾ tsp cumin, garlic and cook for about half a minute or until fragrant.
- Spoon in lime juice.
- Arrange in a bowl and wrap with foil to keep warm.
- Make diagonal slices of chicken thighs and put onto platters.
- Prepare tortilla by following the directions on the package.
- Stuff few slices of chicken in each tortilla alongside cheese and onion mixture.
- Wrap tortilla and serve.

12. Classic Pico De Gallo

Ingredients:

- ¼ cup chopped fresh cilantro
- 1 cup small-diced white or sweet onion
- 1/3 cup fresh lime juice
- 2-3 serrano chiles, stemmed and finely chopped
- 4 cups seeded and diced fresh tomatoes
- Kosher salt

Directions

- Take a bowl; add 2 tsp salt, cilantro, serranos, lime juice, onion, tomatoes and combine.
- Mix, cover and let it stand for about 60 minutes on room temperature.
- Flavor with salt (if desired).
- Let it chill in refrigerator for about 3 days before you strain and serve.

13. Migas (Scrambled Eggs With Corn Tortillas)

Ingredients:

- ¼ tsp freshly ground black pepper
- ½ cup Chipotle Sour Cream
- ½ cup Salsa
- ½ cup thinly sliced scallions
- ½ tsp kosher salt
- ¾ cup finely diced bell peppers
- 1 small to medium yellow onion, finely diced (¾ cup)
- 1-½ cups shredded Monterey Jack or pepper Jack cheese
- 12 large eggs, beaten
- 4 (6-inch) corn tortillas sliced into long, narrow strips
- 4 Tbsp (½ stick) unsalted butter

Directions

- Add peppers, onions to saucepan coated with melted butter and cook for about 3 minutes onto medium-high heat or until softens.
- Add tortillas and cook for about 4-5 more minutes or until slightly golden.
- Flavor with pepper and salt.

- Decant eggs in tortilla mixture and cook until eggs a properly cooked but a little wet, spoon often.
- Add cheese and spoon to mix with runny eggs.
- Distribute among platter; add 1 tbsp salsa and dollop sour cream topping.
- Splash with scallions and serve.

14. Avocado, Mango And Pineapple Salad With Pistachios And Pickled Shallots

Ingredients:

- ¼ cup roasted, salted pistachios, coarsely chopped
- ½ medium pineapple, peeled, cored, and sliced into ½ inch dice
- 1 medium mango seeded, peeled, and sliced lengthwise ¼ inch thick
- 1 medium shallot, sliced into very thin rings
- 1 tbsp thinly sliced fresh basil
- 1 tbsp thinly sliced fresh mint
- 1 tsp red vinegar
- 2 cups baby arugula or watercress
- 2 kiwis, peeled, halved, and sliced ¼ inch thick
- 2 Tbsp vinegar
- 3 medium firm-ripe avocados, pitted, peeled, and sliced lengthwise ¼-inch thick
- 3 Tbsp extra-virgin olive oil
- Freshly ground black pepper
- Kosher salt

Directions

- Take a bowl; add a pinch of salt, vinegar alongside shallot and toss to coat.
- Keep it aside for about 15 minutes, spoon once.
- Drain shallow and keep vinegar for later use.
- Combine shallot vinegar, red vinegar alongside olive oil and whisk.
- Take another bowl; add few grinds of pepper, ¼ tsp salt, basil, mint, pistachios, watercress or arugula, pickled shallots, 1 tbsp vinaigrette and toss to combine.
- Place pineapple, mango, kiwi, avocado on platter, splash remaining vinaigrette and flavor with pepper as well as salt.
- Add arugula mixture topping and serve.

15. Spicy Grilled Corn Salad With Black Beans And Queso Fresco

Ingredients:

- ¼ cup chopped fresh cilantro
- ½ cup olive oil
- 1 15-½ oz can black beans, drained and rinsed
- 1 large red bell pepper
- 1 medium red onion, sliced into disks about 1/3 inch thick
- 1 small canned chipotle, seeded and minced, plus 1 tbsp adobo sauce
- 1 tbsp chopped fresh oregano
- 2 Tbsp vinegar
- 3 ears fresh corn, husked
- 5 oz queso fresco or feta, crumbled
- Kosher salt and freshly ground black pepper

Directions
- Prepare the grill.
- Place pepper, onion, corn on to baking sheet and rub with 2 tbsp of oil.
- Flavor with ½ tsp pepper and 1 tsp salt.
- Grill onion as well as corn for about 8-10 minutes or until brown, flip often.

- Arrange onto cutting board and let it cool.
- Grill for about 12 minutes or until charred.
- Put pepper in a bowl, cover and let it cool.
- In the meantime; take a bowl, add ½ tsp pepper, 1 tsp salt, vinegar, chipotle and adobo sauce, 6 tbsp oil and whisk.
- Take another bowl; add chopped onion and cobs to it.
- Chop and remove seeds from pepper.
- Add it to a bowl alongside oregano, cilantro, cheese and beans.
- Whisk dressing again and combine with corn mixture.
- Flavor with pepper and salt before you serve.

16. Cube Steak With Lime Mojo

Ingredients:

- ½ cup fresh orange juice
- ½ large red bell pepper, cored and thinly sliced
- ½ large white onion, thinly sliced
- ¾ cup fresh lime juice
- 1 tbsp canola oil
- 1 tsp granulated sugar
- 1 tsp ground cumin
- 1-½ tsp finely chopped fresh oregano
- 4 beef cube steaks
- 8 medium cloves garlic, peeled
- Freshly ground black pepper
- Kosher salt

Directions

- Add 2 tsp salt onto crushed garlic and let it stand for about 10 minutes.
- Add ½ tsp black pepper, cumin as well as oregano to form paste.
- Arrange it in a bowl, add sugar, orange juice, lime juice and whisk to combine.
- Add steak to skillet, pour garlic mixture onto it and let it stand for about 15 minutes.

- In the mean time, add pepper, onions to skillet coated with heated oil and cook for about 3 minutes or until softens, spoon frequently.
- Arrange in a bowl.
- Add steaks to pan alongside 2 tbsp mojo and cook for about 2 minutes.
- Turn, add peppers, onions and cook for about a minute (covered).
- Cook for about 3 minutes (uncovered) and serve with pepper, onions topping alongside drizzled cooked mojo. '

17. Breakfast Burrito

Ingredients:

- ½ cup sliced cilantro
- ¾ tsp salt, divided
- 4 (10-12) inch flour tortillas
- 1 cup sliced white onion
- 1 cup grated Monterey Jack cheese
- 1 large tomato, sliced
- 1 ripe avocado, peeled, chopped, pitted and quartered
- 2 canned chipotles en adobo, sliced
- 2 Tbsp Mexican crema or milk
- 4 Tbsp vegetable oil, divided
- 8 large eggs
- 2 cans about 15 oz, pinto or black beans, washed and drained

Directions

- Prepare oven at 350 F.
- Heat tortilla for about 10 minutes in oven and wrap with foil to keep it warm.
- Meanwhile, add onion to skillet coated with 2 tbsp heated oil and cook for about 8 minutes on medium heat or until golden, spoon.

- Add ½ tsp salt, beans, chipotles, tomatoes and cook for about 5 more minutes, spoon until thoroughly heated.
- Scramble eggs in skillet and add crema or milk afterwards.
- Cook until curds and flavor with ¼ tsp salt.
- Separate when moist.
- Add ¼ sliced cilantro, ¼ chopped avocado, ¼ cheese, ¼ bean mixture, ¼ eggs onto flat tortilla and wrap.
- Do the same for remaining tortillas before you serve burritos.

18. Spicy Cilantro Chicken Wings

Ingredients:

- ½ stick unsalted butter, melted
- ½ tsp black pepper
- 1 hot green chile, such as habanero, serrano, or Thai, chopped
- 1 large garlic clove, chopped
- 1/3 cup chopped cilantro stems
- 1-½ tsp finely grated lime zest
- 1-¾ tsp kosher salt
- 2 Tbsp Worcestershire sauce
- 3 lb chicken wings
- 3 Tbsp lime juice
- About 4 cups vegetable oil for frying
- Cilantro leaves

Directions

- Add pepper, ¾ tsp salt, garlic, chili, worcestershire, juice, lime zest, cilantro stems to food processor and process until smooth.
- Add butter half way through until properly incorporated.
- Arrange to a sauce bowl.
- Use paper sheet to pat dry wings and halve them.
- Flavor with remaining 1 tsp salt.

- Add wings to skillet coated with heated oil and cook for about 10 minutes per batch or until golden.
- Arrange wings in a bowl alongside toss and toss to combine or serve on side (if desired).
- Arrange wings onto platter, splash with cilantro leaves and serve alongside sauce on the side.

19. Smoky Corn Quesadillas

Ingredients:

- ¼ cup fresh corn kernels
- ½ cup grated Monterey Jack
- ½ tsp smoked paprika
- 2 7-8-inch flour tortillas
- 2 Tbsp chopped fresh cilantro
- 2 tsp vegetable oil
- Kosher salt
- Lime wedges and sour cream, for serving

Directions

- Take a bowl; add 1/8 tsp salt, paprika, cilantro, monterey jack, corn and combine.
- Distribute mixture uniformly between tortilla, spread onto each half and wrap.
- Add quesadillas to skillet coated with heated oil and cook for about 2 minutes or until golden and crisp.
- Turn and cook for about 2 more minutes until crisp.
- Set aside to cool, chop in wedges and serve alongside sour cream.

20. Black Pepper Crusted Beef Tenderloin With Chimichurri Sauce

Ingredients:

For the chimichurri sauce

- ¼ tsp crushed red pepper flakes
- 1 tbsp chopped garlic
- 1 tbsp fresh oregano or 1 tsp dried
- 1 tbsp red vinegar
- 1 tsp fresh lime juice; more to taste
- 1/3 cup extra-virgin olive oil
- 1-½ oz mixed fresh cilantro and flat-leaf parsley leaves
- Kosher salt

For the steaks

- 1 tbsp olive oil
- 2 Tbsp black peppercorns, coarsely crushed
- 4 6-7-oz beef tenderloin steaks, about 1-½ inches thick
- Kosher or coarse salt

Directions

- Add garlic, oregano, parsley, cilantro to food processor and process until thinly sliced.
- Arrange mixture in a bowl, spoon in ½ tsp salt, red pepper flakes, lime juice, vinegar and olive oil to make sauce.
- Take a bowl; add 2 tsp salt alongside crushed peppercorns to combine.
- Rub mixture on both sides of the steak and coat well.
- Keep it aside for about half an hour to 45 minutes on room temperature.
- Prepare oven at 350 F.
- Add steaks to skillet coated with heated oil and cook for about 4 minutes onto medium-high heat or until golden.
- Turn, cook for about 4 more minutes or until brown.
- Shift skillet to oven and cook for about 5-6 minutes or until medium rare.
- Cool for a while and serve with chimichurri sauce topping.

21. Seared Tilapia With Spicy Orange Salsa

Ingredients:

- ½ cup coarsely chopped fresh cilantro
- ½ cup small-diced red onion
- 1 fresh serrano or jalapeño chile, minced
- 1 tsp ground cumin
- 2 Tbsp fresh lime juice
- 2 Tbsp mild olive oil
- 4 5-oz tilapia fillets
- 4 medium navel oranges
- Freshly ground black pepper
- Kosher salt

Directions
- Expose round flesh of oranges by chopping.
- Peel and remove membrane from the orange.
- Squeeze oranges over the bowl to get the remaining juice.
- Chop in 4 crosswise pieces and return it back to bowl.
- Add1 tsp salt, cumin, lime juice, cilantro, onion and spoon to combine.
- Add chili to taste and spoon.

- Let it stand for about 12 minutes to blend the flavors.
- Use paper sheet to pat dry fish and flavor with pepper as well as salt.
- Add fillets to skillet coated with heated oil and cook for about 3 minutes or until browned.
- Flip and continue cooking for about 2 more minutes or until browned.
- Drain and arrange onto platters.
- Repeat the process for remaining fish fillets and serve with salsa topping.

22. Brazilian Skirt Steak With Golden Garlic Butter

Ingredients:

- 1 tbsp chopped fresh flat-leaf parsley
- 1-½ lb skirt steak, trimmed and sliced into 4 pieces
- 2 oz unsalted butter
- 2 Tbsp canola oil or vegetable oil
- 6 medium cloves garlic
- Freshly ground black pepper
- Kosher salt

Directions

- Peel and smash garlic, splash with salt and mince.
- Use paper sheet to pat dry steak and generously flavor with pepper and salt.
- Add steak to skillet coated with heated oil and cook for about 4 minutes onto medium-high or until medium rare.
- Arrange steak onto platter and keep it aside.
- Add garlic to skillet coated with melted butter and cook for about 5 minutes or until golden.
- Chop steak and place in platters.
- Rub garlic butter onto steak and serve with splashed parsley.

23. Grilled Steak Tacos With Spicy Slaw

Ingredients:

- ½ cup sour cream
- 1-¼ lb flank steak
- 1-½ tsp pure ancho chile powder
- Kosher salt and freshly ground black pepper
- Lime wedges for serving
- 1 large red onion, sliced in half inch rounds
- 1 tbsp fresh lime juice
- 2 Tbsp olive oil
- 2 tsp granulated sugar
- 1 to 2 medium jalapeños, stemmed
- 3 cups thinly sliced green cabbage
- 8 corn tortillas

Directions

- Prepare grill at 375 F.
- In the meantime; take a bowl, add ¾ tsp pepper, 2 tsp salt, 1 tsp sugar alongside ancho powder and combine.
- Use paper sheet to pat dry steak and rub ancho mixture on both sides.

- Let it stand for a while on room temperature while heating the grill.
- Place jalapenos as well as onion rounds on platter, splash with ½ tsp pepper, ½ tsp salt and 1 tbsp oil.
- Take another bowl; add ½ tsp salt, 1 tsp sugar, lime juice alongside cabbage and toss.
- Add remaining 1 tbsp oil and toss to combine.
- Place jalapenos, onion as well as steak on the grate and grill for about 12-14 minutes or until medium rare.
- Flip half way through.
- Separate veggies, steak and let it cool for a bit before you chop.
- Add thinly sliced jalapeno, onion to cabbage mixture and toss to combine.
- Flavor with lime juice, pepper and salt.
- Scatter tortillas onto grill and heat for about 2 minutes or until softens, flip once.
- Repeat the process for remaining tortillas.
- Finely chop steak and stuff between tortillas.
- Add dollop sour cream and slaw topping.
- Serve alongside lime wedges.

24. Grilled Portobello Quesadillas

Ingredients:

- 2 oz feta cheese, crumbled
- 4 10-inch flour tortillas
- 4 medium scallions, thinly sliced
- 4 oz pepper Jack cheese, grated
- 6 medium portobello caps, wiped clean with a damp towel and gills scraped
- Kosher salt and freshly ground black pepper
- Olive oil

Directions

- Prepare grill at 425-450 F.
- Rub oil on both sides or portobellos and flavor with pepper as well as salt.
- Grill portobellos for about 7 minutes and flip half way through.
- Finely chop portobellos.
- Arrange tortilla onto skillet with medium heat; splash cheeses, scallions and potobellos onto it.
- Add another tortilla topping and press with spatula.
- Cook for about 8 minutes or until browned, flip once.

- Arrange in platter and repeat the same process for remaining tortillas before you serve with sliced quesadillas wedges.

25. Grilled Chicken With Curried Couscous, Spinach And Mango

Ingredients:

- ¼ cup slivered almonds, toasted
- 1 cup whole-wheat couscous
- 1 small firm-ripe mango, sliced into ½ inch dice
- 1 tbsp finely chopped fresh flat-leaf parsley
- 1 tbsp thinly sliced shallot
- 1 tsp curry powder
- 2 oz baby spinach
- 3 Tbsp white vinegar
- 4 boneless, skinless chicken breast halves (each 6-7 oz)
- 5 Tbsp + 1 tsp extra-virgin olive oil
- Kosher salt and freshly ground black pepper

Directions

- Prepare grill at 375 F.
- Add shallot to skillet coated with 1 tbsp heated olive oil and cook for about 2 minutes or until translucent, spoon.
- Add curry powder and cook for about half a minute more or until fragrant, spoon.
- Spoon in 3 tbsp olive oil as well as vinegar.

- Separate it from heat, flavor with pepper as well as salt.
- Grill chicken (coated with ¼ tsp salt, few grinds pepper and 1 tbsp olive oil) for about 13-15 minutes or until thoroughly cooked.
- Arrange onto platter.
- In the meantime, add ½ tsp salt alongside 1 cup water to skillet and boil.
- Take an heatproof bowl; add couscous, 1 tsp olive oil and toss to combine.
- Put boiling water onto couscous and spoon.
- Cover and let it stand for about 6 minutes before you fluff with fork.
- Add parsley, almonds, mango, 3 tbsp vinaigrette and toss.
- Flavor with pepper and salt.
- Coat spinach with vinaigrette.
- Distribute couscous equally among platters.
- Add chicken, spinach topping and serve with remaining drizzled vinaigrette.

26. Sofrito Scallops With Saffron Rice

Ingredients:

- ½ tsp ground cumin
- 1 8-oz can tomato sauce
- 1 lb bay scallops
- 1 medium yellow onion, finely chopped
- 1 small green bell pepper, finely chopped
- 1 tbsp ketchup
- 1 tsp finely chopped fresh oregano
- 1-½ cups long-grain white rice
- 3 medium cloves garlic, minced
- 3 Tbsp extra-virgin olive oil
- Freshly ground black pepper
- Kosher salt
- Pinch of saffron threads
- Vinegar, ½ cup

Directions

- Add saffron to skillet coated with 1 tbsp heated oil and heat until sizzled.
- Add rice and spoon.
- Add 1 ½ tsp salt, 3 cups of water and bring to boil for about a minute.

- Spoon once, cover and let it cook onto low heat for about 18 minutes or until water absorbs or rice is tender.
- In the mean time, add garlic, green pepper, onion to skillet coated with remaining 2 tbsp heated oil and cook for about 10 minutes or until veggies are softens.
- Spoon in ½ tsp pepper, 1 tsp salt, cumin and oregano.
- Add vinegar and simmer for about 4 minutes on low heat.
- Spoon in a cup water alongside tomato sauce and bring to boil.
- Cover and let it cook for about 8 minutes on low heat or until thickens.
- Spoon in ketchup and flavor with pepper and salt.
- Cook hot sofrito and scallops for about 4 minutes or until thoroughly cooked, spoon often.
- Arrange rice onto platter and add scallop mixture topping.
- Flavor with lemon juice before you serve.

27. Spinach And Tomatilla Guacamole

Ingredients:

- ¼ cup coarsely chopped cilantro
- ½ cup finely chopped white onion
- 1 small tomato, chopped
- 1 tbsp extra-virgin olive oil
- 1 tbsp fresh lime juice; more to taste
- 2 coarsely chopped medium Hass avocados
- 2 medium tomatillos, husked and chopped
- 2 oz baby spinach
- Kosher salt

Directions

- Add tomatillos, oil, spinach to food processor and process until puree.
- Decant any liquid, and put the mixture in a bowl.
- Spoon in 1 ½ tsp salt, lime juice, cilantro, onion, tomato and avocados.
- Flavor with more salt as well as lime juice (if desired) before you serve.

28. Tomatillo Gazpacho

Ingredients:

- ¼ small red onion, finely diced
- ½ large red bell pepper, sliced into small dice
- ½ seedless English cucumber, sliced into small dice
- 1 lb tomatillos, husked, rinsed, and sliced into medium dice
- 1 medium clove garlic, minced
- 1 tbsp fresh lime juice; more as needed
- 2 medium avocados, sliced into small dice
- 2 Tbsp chopped fresh cilantro
- 2 Tbsp extra-virgin olive oil
- Kosher salt and freshly ground black pepper
- One 14-oz can low-salt chicken broth

Directions

- Add garlic, tomatillos to saucepan coated with broth and boil onto reduced heat until tomatillos are thoroughly cooked.
- Set aside to cool for about 10 minutes.
- Add mixture to food processor alongside olive oil and process well.
- Arrange puree in a pan and chill in refrigerator.
- After puree is cooled, spoon in lime juice, cilantro, onion, bell pepper, cucumber and avocado.

- Flavor with pepper as well as salt.
- Let it chill for about 2-4 hours.
- Adjust seasoning before you serve.

29. Southwestern Rice Pilaf

Ingredients:

- ½ cup coarsely chopped fresh cilantro
- 1 14-oz can diced tomatoes, drained well
- 1 jalapeño, stemmed, seeded, and minced
- 1 lime
- 1 medium onion, medium diced
- 1 medium poblano, stemmed, seeded, and finely diced
- 1 tsp ground cumin
- 1 tsp kosher salt; more as needed
- 1-½ cups long-grain white rice
- 1-½ tsp chili powder
- 2 Tbsp extra-virgin olive oil
- 2-½ cups low-salt chicken broth
- 2 tbsp large cloves garlic, minced

Directions

- Add garlic, poblano, onion to skillet coated with heated oil and cook for about 4 minutes onto reduced heat, spoon often.
- Add cumin, chili powder and cook for about 4 more minutes or until spices are fragrant, spoon constantly.
- Add salt, rice and spoon to coat.

- Toast for about 6 minutes and spoon constantly to keep the grain separated.
- Add tomatoes, chicken broth, spoon once and bring to boil.
- Cover and cook for about 20 minutes on reduced heat.
- Separate it from the heat and let it stand for a while to cool.
- In the meantime, grate 1 tbsp zest from lime and make wedges.
- Fluff rice using fork and fold lime zest, jalapeno, cilantro in pilaf.
- Flavor with salt and serve alongside lime wedges onto rice.

30. Grilled Chicken With Tomato, Lime And Cilantro Salsa

Ingredients:

- ½ cup finely chopped fresh cilantro
- 1-½ to 2 tsp granulated sugar
- 2 cups seeded, diced ripe tomatoes
- 2 Tbsp fresh lime juice
- 2 tsp minced chipotle
- 3 Tbsp extra-virgin olive oil
- 4 boneless, skinless chicken breast halves
- 4 scallions, thinly sliced
- Finely grated zest of 1 lime
- Kosher salt and freshly ground black pepper

Directions
- Prepare grill onto 375 to 400 F.
- Take a bowl; add lime zest, 1 ½ tsp sugar, 1 tbsp oil, lime juice scallions, cilantro, tomatoes and combine.
- Take another bowl; add ¼ tsp pepper, ½ tsp salt, remaining 2 tbsp oil, chipotle and combine.
- Trim chicken in a pound with ½ inch thickness.
- Add chicken to chipotle mixture and toss to combine.

- Place chicken on grate and grill (covered) for about 4 minutes or until turns opaque.
- Flip and cook for about 4 more minutes.
- Arrange chicken onto cutting board and let it cool before you chop in ½ inch diagonal slices.
- Place chicken onto platter and serve with salsa topping.

Roasted Pork Loin

Country: Brazil

Ingredients
- 1 4 1/2 to 5 lb loin of pork (10 chops)
- 2 teaspoons salt
- freshly ground pepper
- 1 cup orange juice
- 1/2 cup light brown sugar
- 1 tablespoon ginger
- 1/4 teaspoon cloves

Directions
- Preheat oven to 325F. Place pork, fat side up, in a roasting pan.
- Insert thermometer, do not let it touch bone.
- Roast for 35 minutes to the pound, or until it reaches 170F.
- In a small saucepan, mix the orange juice, sugar, ginger & cloves.
- Simmer for 30 minutes. Brush this glaze at least twice over the pork while it is roasting.

Steaks – Portuguese Style

Country: Brazil

Ingredients
- 4 Medium Sirloin Steak
- 4 Cloves Garlic - Chopped
- 1/4 Cup Olive Oil
- 1 Can Tomatoes - Chopped
- 1 Medium Onion - Chopped
- 1 Medium Bell Pepper - Chopped
- 6 Large New Potatoes - Boiled And Sliced
- Olives — For Garnish
- Bread Or Toast

Directions
- Season steaks with garlic and salt. Let stand 10 minutes.
- Heat oil, add tomatoes, onion and green pepper. Sauté for 10 minutes.
- Add steaks and brown deeply on both sides. Cover the skillet and cook over low heat for 15 minutes. Add potatoes and olives and heat through. Serve with bread or toast to pick up the sauce.

Lemon Chimichurri

Country: Argentina

Ingredients
- 120ml/4fl.oz. Olive Oil
- 90ml/3fl.oz. Lemon Juice
- 1 tbsp freshly chopped Parsley
- 1 tbsp freshly chopped Thyme
- 1 Garlic Clove, Crushed
- 2 Shallots, finely chopped
- Salt and pepper to taste

Directions
- Place all the ingredients in a blender and process until well blended and relatively smooth.
- Cover and leave to stand for at least 2 hours at room temperature before serving.

Famous Meat-Filled Empanadas

Country: Argentina

Ingredients
- 1/2 cup shortening
- 2 onions, chopped

- 1 pound lean ground beef
- 2 teaspoons Hungarian sweet paprika
- 3/4 teaspoon hot paprika
- 1/2 teaspoon crushed red pepper flakes
- 1 teaspoon ground cumin
- 1 tablespoon distilled white vinegar
- 1/4 cup raisins
- 1/2 cup pitted green olives, chopped
- 2 hard-cooked eggs, chopped
- salt to taste
- 1 (17.5 ounce) package frozen puff pastry sheets, thawed

Directions
- In a sauté; pan melt the shortening and add the chopped onions. Cook the onions until just before they begin to turn golden. Remove from the heat and stir in the sweet paprika, hot paprika, crushed red pepper flakes and salt to taste.
- Spread the meat on a sieve and pour boiling water on it for partial cooking. Allow meat to cool. Place meat in a dish and add salt to taste, cumin and vinegar. Mix and add the meat to the onion mixture. Mix well and place on a flat to dish to cool and harden.
- Cut puff pastry dough into 10 round shells. Place a spoonful of the meat mixture on each round; add some of the raisins, olives and hard-boiled egg. Avoid reaching the edges of the pastry with the filling because its oiliness will prevent good sealing.

- Slightly wet the edge of the pastry, fold in two and stick edges together. The shape should resemble that of a half-moon. You should have a 2/3 to 1/2 inch flat edge of pastry to work with.
- Seal by twisting edge, step by step, between thumb and index finger, making sure to add pressure before releasing the pinch and moving on to the next curl. Other sealing procedures like pinching without curling or using a fork to seal will not prevent juice leaks during baking, and empanadas must be juicy.
- Preheat oven to 350 degrees F (180 degrees C). Place empanadas on a parchment paper lined baking sheet. Be sure to prick each empanada with a fork near the curl to allow steam to escape during baking. Glaze with egg for shine and bake until golden, about 20 to 30 minutes.

Potato Cake Recipe – LLapingachos

Country: Ecuador

Ingredients
- 4 pounds white potatoes
- 1 onion, chopped fine
- 2 tablespoons achiote oil
- 1 egg yolk
- 1 cup shredded white cheese (queso fresco, farmer's cheese, or mozzarella)

- 4 green onions, minced
- Salt and pepper to taste
- Peanut sauce

Directions
- Peel the potatoes and add them to a large pot of boiling salted water. Cook until tender when pierced with a fork.
- While the potatoes are cooking, sauté the onion in the achiote oil until soft. Set aside to cool.
- Whip the boiled potatoes in a standing mixer to mashed them, or run them through a ricer. Season with salt and pepper to taste. (If using paprika instead of achiote oil, mix the paprika in with the mashed potatoes).
- Mix the cooked onions and the egg yolk in with potatoes. Chill potato mixture for at least two hours, or overnight.
- Mix the grated cheese with the minced green onions.
- Shape the mashed potato mixture into balls slightly larger than a golf ball. Make a large hole with your finger in the middle, and press about a tablespoon of the cheese mixture into the hole.
- Close the mashed potato mixture over the cheese center, and then gently pat the ball into a pancake about a half inch thick. Chill the pancakes for 30 minutes.
- Heat 3 to 4 tablespoons of vegetable oil in a skillet. Fry the pancakes in batches, about 3 minutes on each side.

Keep pancakes warm in a 200- degree oven until ready to serve. Serve with peanut sauce.

Valdiviano (Beef Jerky And Onion Soup)

Country: Chile

Ingredients

- 3 Tablespoons Olive Oil
- 4 Large Onion - Chopped
- 2 Tablespoons Paprika
- 1 Small Winter Squash - Chopped
- 1/2 Pound Beef Jerky - Chopped
- 1 Teaspoon Cumin
- 1 Teaspoon Oregano
- 6 Cups Beef Broth
- Salt And Pepper
- 8 Medium Eggs
- 2 Tablespoons Parsley - Chopped
- 1 Lemon Juice
- 1 Orange Juice

Directions
- Sauté onion, squash and paprika in oil for 10 minutes. Add jerky, cumin, oregano and broth.

- Simmer for 25 minutes. Season with salt and pepper. Poach eggs in water for 5 minutes.
- Stir in lemon juice and orange juice to the soup. Simmer for 1 minute.
- Place an egg in a soup bowl, top with soup and sprinkle with parsley. Serve.

Tomatican Con Pulpa De Cerdo (Corn And Pork Stew)

Country: Chile

Ingredients
- 3 Tablespoons Olive Oil
- 2 Pounds Pork - Cubed
- Salt And Pepper
- 2 Large Onion - Sliced
- 3 Cloves Garlic - Chopped
- 1 Teaspoon Cumin
- 2 Teaspoons Oregano
- 3 Cans Tomatoes - Chopped
- 1 Cup Corn
- 1 Tablespoon Parsley - Chopped
- 1/2 Bunch Cilantro - Chopped
- 1 Medium Jalapeno - Chopped

Directions

- Sautépork in oil, for 10 minutes. Season with salt and pepper, add onions, sauté 8 minutes, add garlic, cumin, oregano, and tomatoes, simmer 45 minutes.
- Add corn, cilantro, parsley and jalapeno, simmer 15 minutes and serve.

Spicy Crab Cakes

Country: Chile

Ingredients
- 1/2 Pound Crab Meat - precooked
- 1 Small White Onions - chopped and sautéd
- 1 Large Egg - beaten
- 1/2 Lemon Juice
- Pepper - to taste
- 1 Pinch Spanish Paprika
- 1/2 Cup Flour
- 1 Teaspoon Aji Paste
- 1 Tablespoon Unsalted Butter - melted
- 1 1/2 Cups Fine Bread Crumbs
- 1/2 Cup Corn Oil
- 2 Tablespoons Mayonnaise - homemade

Directions
- In a glass bowl, mix crab meat, onion, egg, lemon juice, pepper, paprika, aji paste, flour, and butter.

- Mix well. Form cakes into 2 inch diameter cakes and refrigerate for 1 hour.
- Place on individual wax paper squares. Coat cakes in bread crumbs and fry in hot oil until golden brown on both sides.
- Serve hot with a dollop of mayonnaise on top.

Pastel De Zapallitos

Country: Chile

Ingredients
- 1 Cup Bread Crumbs
- 1 Cup Milk
- 6 Medium Zucchini
- 1 Cup Beef Stock Or Water
- 1 Medium Onion - finely chopped
- 3 Cloves Garlic - finely chopped
- 3 Tablespoons Olive Oil
- 2 Medium Eggs - beaten
- 1 Cup Parmesan Cheese - grated
- Salt And Pepper - to taste
- 1/2 Cup Bread Crumbs

Directions
- Preheat oven to 375*. Soak bread in milk 5 minutes. Blanche zucchini in boiling stock 5 minutes. Remove

zucchini, reduce stock to 1/2 cup. Add to bread mixture.

- Sauté onion and garlic in oil. Add bread mixture, zucchini, eggs, 1/2 cheese, salt and pepper.
- Simmer 5 minutes. Spread into buttered baking dish.
- Sprinkle with remaining cheese and bread crumbs, bake 30 minutes.

Shrimp And Fish Stew

Country: Peru

Ingredients
- 2 Tablespoons Olive Oil
- 1 Medium Onion - finely chopped
- 2 Cloves Garlic - finely chopped
- 3 Tablespoons Tomato Sauce
- 6 Cups Fish Broth - or chicken
- 1/2 Cup Green Peas
- 1/2 Cup Corn
- 2 Large Potatoes - peeled and cubed
- 1 Teaspoon Salt
- 2 Teaspoons Aji Chile Powder - or new Mexican
- 1 Teaspoon Marjoram
- 3 Ounces Cream Cheese
- 2 Cups Milk
- 24 Large Shrimp - shelled
- 4 Medium Eggs - lightly beaten

- 6 Fillets Halibut - or cod or sole

Directions
- Heat oil in large pan and sauté garlic and onion. Add tomato sauce, fish broth, peas, corn, potatoes, salt, chile powder, and marjoram.
- Bring to a simmer and cook covered for 20 minutes. Beat the cream cheese until soft and add it bit by bit to the soup, stirring constantly.
- Stir in milk and bring to a simmer. Add shrimp and cook for 3 minutes. Remove from heat. Gradually add 2 cups of hot soup to the eggs, stirring constantly.
- Pour egg mixture back into the soup and reheat over low heat. Meanwhile fry fish in skillet until done, about 3 minutes per side.
- Place a piece of fried fish in each soup bowl and ladle soup over it.

Peruvian Garlic Chicken

Country: Peru

Ingredients
- 1/2 Cup Olive Oil
- 3 Medium Onions - chopped
- 6 Cloves Garlic - chopped
- 4 Medium Chopped Rocoto Chiles - or jalapenos

- 1/2 Teaspoon Cinnamon
- 1 Tablespoon Cumin
- 1 Teaspoon Basil
- 2 Cups Peanuts - roasted and chopped
- 1/2 Cup Parmesan Cheese
- 3 Pounds Chicken Breasts - chopped
- 3/4 Cup Lowfat Yogurt - room Temp.
- Salt And Pepper
- Boiled Potatoes - for garnish

Directions

1. Heatoil in large saucepan and sauté onions and garlic until the onions are soft.
2. Add chiles, cinnamon, cumin, basil, peanuts, cheese, and chicken. stir well.
3. Simmer for 30 minutes or until chicken is done. 2 minutes before serving, add yogurt and stir well.
4. Serve surrounded by potatoes.

Pork With Lemon

Country: Peru

Ingredients
- 2 Pounds Pork - cubed
- 2 Tablespoons Flour
- 1/4 Cup Olive Oil
- 1 Tablespoon Fresh Ginger Root - grated
- 1 Large Onion - thinly sliced
- 3 Medium Tomatoes - chopped
- 4 Medium Jalapeno - chopped
- 2 Tablespoons Parsley - finely chopped
- 1/2 Teaspoon Lemon Peel - grated
- 1/2 Cup Lemon Juice
- 2 Cups Chicken Stock
- Lemon Wedges - for garnish
- Parsley - for garnish

Directions
- Sprinkle pork with flour. Heat the oil and sauté meat with the ginger until pork is nicely browned.
- Add onion, tomatoes, and chiles. Cook for 3 minutes. Add parsley, lemon peel, lemon juice and stock.

- Reduce heat and simmer uncovered for 20 minutes and stock is reduced to the consistency of gravy.
- Serve with rice or boiled potatoes, garnished with lemon wedges and parsley

Garlic Pork

Country: Guyana

Ingredients
- 3 to 4 pounds pork loin, cut into 1-inch pieces 3 cups white vinegar
- 1/2 pound garlic, separated into cloves and peeled 4 stalks
- fresh thyme or 1 teaspoon dried
- 6 to 8 wiri wiri-type peppers (or 2 scotch bonnet-type peppers)
- 2 cups cold water
- 2 teaspoons salt
- 6 cloves
- 1 tablespoon vegetable oil

Directions
- In a large bowl, wash the pork pieces with 1 cup of the vinegar. Lift them from the bowl with 2 large forks; do not use your hands.

- Place the pork in a large jar or bottle.
  Place the peeled garlic, thyme, and chilies in a mortar and pound to a paste. Then add the cold water and the remaining 2 cups of vinegar to the garlic mixture.
- Add the salt and cloves and pour the garlic and vinegar mixture over the pork, making sure that the pork is completely covered.
- Tightly cover the jar and allow the pork to marinate in a cool place for 3 to 4 days or longer.
- To cook, place the pork in a heavy skillet and cook until the liquid evaporates. Then add the vegetable oil and fry the pork until it is brown.
- Serve hot – with bread, or over white rice. Our family has always served with shots of Gin, Vodka or Whiskey

Pepperpot

Country: Guyana

Ingredients
- 1 lb. oxtail, or pig's tail, cut into joints
- 1 cow's heel, quartered
- 2 lb. lean pork or beef, or both, cut into 2-inch cubes
- 1 stewing chicken, cut into serving pieces
- 1/2/ lb. salt beef
- 1 lime
- 6 tablespoons casareep*
- 1 Stick cinnamon (optional)

- 3 cloves
- 2 or 3 hot peppers (tied in cheesecloth if they are to be removed after cooking)
- 2 tablespoons Demerara brown sugar.
- Salt

Directions
- Wash the meats well with lime juice
- Boil the cow's heel with enough water to cover the meat. When half-cooked, about 1 hour, add the other meats and casareep. Simmer for another hour.
- Add the remaining ingredients: simmer gently until the meats are tender and the sauce is thick, about 1 hour. Remove the hot peppers before serving (optional).

* What is a Cassareep? Cassareep is the juice of cassava boiled until it reduces and caramelizes. It is the creation of the Guyanese Amerindian (Indigenous Peoples) and is made from the juice of the bitter cassava. The juice is boiled long and slowly to remove any poisonous elements and impurities. The result is a thick brown liquid, cassareep. It is used to cook many Guyana's dishes.

Yum-Yums

Country: Guyana

Ingredients
- 4 oz short crust pastry
- 4 oz margarine
- 4 oz sugar
- 2 eggs
- 4 oz flour
- ½ tsp baking powder
- Grated lemon rind (of 1 lemon), or 1 tsp vanilla essence
- 1 tbsp jam

Directions
- Line 10 or 12 patty or muffin pan forms with thinly rolled pastry.
- Put a little jam in each.
- Prepare the cake mixture by the creaming method.
- Put some cake mixture in each lined patty pan.
- Bake for about 20 minutes in a moderate oven at 370°F, and dredge with icing sugar when finished.

Breadfruit Cheese Pie

Country: Guyana

Ingredients
- ½ medium sized breadfruit
- ½ lb cheese
- 2 tbs. mustard

- 1 tsp. salt
- 1 tbs. bread crumbs
- 2 tbs. flour
- ½ oz margarine
- 1¾ cups milk or water 1 egg (optional)

Directions
<u>What is breadfruit?</u>

- Wash breadfruit and cut into pieces lengthwise. Peel and remove core. Boil in salted water. Grate cheese and grease a pie dish. Grate cheese and mix with milk, flour and margarine to make a sauce. When breadfruit is cooked and cooled, cut into small pieces. Pour the sauce over the breadfruit pieces.
- Stir without breaking breadfruit pieces. Pour the mixture into the pie dish.
- Mix the remainder of the cheese with the bread crumbs. Sprinkle over the top of the pie. Brown in a moderate oven for about 15 minutes.

Stuffed Zucchini (Zapallitos Rellenos)

Country: Uruguay

Ingredients
- 2-3 medium zucchini (courgettes)
- 2 tbl (30 ml) olive oil

- Med onion, finely chopped
- 3/4 cup(180 ml) bread crumbs, preferably fresh
- 1/2 cup(250 ml) milk
- 1 egg, beaten
- Salt and freshly ground pepper to taste
  For the topping:
- 1/4 cup(60 ml) bread crumbs, preferably fresh
- 2 tbl (30 ml) butter, melted

Directions
- Bake the zucchini in a preheated 375F (190C) oven for 30 minutes, until soft but not mushy. Set aside to cool.
- Meanwhile, heat the olive oil in a skillet over moderate heat and sauté the onion until golden brown.
- Combine the bread crumbs, milk, egg, cooked onion, salt, and pepper in a bowl, stirring to combine. Slice the zucchini in two lengthwise and scoop out the pulp.
- Chop the pulp coarsely and stir into the bread crumb mixture. Fill the zucchini shells with the mixture. For the topping, combine the bread crumbs and butter and sprinkle over the zucchini.
- Bake in a preheated 375F (190C) oven until the topping is golden brown, about 25 minutes.

Croquetas de Atún – Tuna Croquettes

Country: Venezuela

Ingredients

- 12 oz. Tuna (1 large can, drained)
- 1 Tomato
- 1 Onion, medium or small
- 1 Garlic Clove, thinly chopped
- 1 Potato, medium to large
- 2 Eggs
- 1 Cup Bread Crumbs
- 2 to 4 Sprigs Cilantro or Parsley, thinly chopped
- 1 Tablespoon Adobo Seasoning
- 1 Tablespoon Worcestershire Sauce
- 2 Cups Oil, for frying

Directions

- Peel the potato and rinse it, place in a large enough pot, cover it by one inch with enough water and boil until fork tender.
- Now you are going to work on a "Sofrito", or a combination of ingredients and condiments cut into very small pieces and sautéed together. For this you are going to use the tomato, the onion, the cilantro (or parsley), and the garlic. You can cut them all as small as possible, or you can even use a processor to chop them up for you.
- Sauté all these ingredients in a large enough pan for about 5 minutes, or until the onions start to brown.
- Drain the tuna and add it to the sofrito in the pan along with the adobo and Worcestershire sauce. Continue to sauté, until the tuna is browned and has mixed with all the other ingredients and all the flavors are absorbed.

- At this point your potato should be done. Remove the pot from the stove and drain the potato. Add the potato into a mixing bowl and mash it. Set aside for it to cool.
- Now your tuna should be ready as well. Remove from the stove, and add the tuna mixture to your mashed potato and mix well.
- Set aside for it to cool down, because you will be handling this mixture with your hands and you don't want it to be too hot.
- Prepare an assembly line next to your stove and add the oil to a frying pan (or deep fryer if you have one), and begin to heat up the oil.
- You should have the bowl with the mixture, a bowl filled with the eggs (scrambled), and a plate with the bread crumbs.
- Grab some of the tuna/potato mix and roll it in your hands to form a croquette in the shape of a "smokie", but don't make them too thick or too thin.
- Place the croquette in the egg bowl and coat with the eggs, then pass it through the bread crumbs and make sure to coat evenly.
- Fry the croquettes until the outside is browned and crispy. Set on paper towels to remove excess oil.
- Serve as an appetizer with tartar sauce, mayo and/or limejuice. Or serve as a main dish accompanied with rice and vegetables.

Crema de Apio – Celery Root Soup

Country: Venezuela

Ingredients
- 500 grams of Apio Venezolano (about 2 to 3 big pieces)
- 4 ¼ cups of Chicken Broth
- Salt

Optional:

- Queso Blanco (Yet another hard to find ingredient)
- 2 tbsp. butter
- ¼ Onion
- Cilantro
- Basil
- Leeks
- Cream Cheese

Directions
- Peel the Apio. Use a knife first for the tougher parts, and then you can use a regular potato peeler for the rest.
- Cut the Apio in half, so that it fits in the pot and the water covers it. This step is optional.
- Cook the Apio and the Chicken Broth in high heat for about 25 minutes, or until the Apio is soft. Just like you would if you where boiling potatoes.
- Add the optional ingredients for extra flavor, such as the onion, cilantro, the basil and the leeks.

- Once the Apio is done, remove the optional ingredients and remove the Apio from the broth.
- Puree the Apio using a food processor and then slowly add the stock little by little until you reach the desired consistency. This is supposed to be a "cream of apio" soup, but if you puree the apio first, and then add the broth bit by bit, mixing well, you can stop adding broth when you have reached the desired consistency, so you don't have a soup that is too thick or too thin. You can also add the optional butter here to help it reach the desired consistency.
- Return the mixture to the pot and cook on low heat for another 10 minutes or so. You can add the remaining broth if it starts to thicken too much.
- Serve with optional cubes of Queso Blanco, or toast, or Cream Cheese, or all three.

Jalapeño Tequeño Poppers

Country: Venezuela

Ingredients
- 1 cup whole wheat flour
- 1 cup all purpose flour
- 1/4 cup butter, softened
- 1 large egg yolk
- 1 teaspoon sugar
- 1/2 teaspoon salt

- 1/2 cup water
- 8 ounces queso blanco, cut in 1 inch cubes
- 6 fresh jalapeños, tops removed
- canola oil

Directions
- In bowl of stand mixer with hook attachment mix flour, butter, egg yolk, sugar, salt and water.
- Knead dough on speed 2 until it separates from bowl. Remove dough from bowl and manually knead on a lightly floured surface until smooth, about 2 minutes.
- Cut dough in half and cover. Roll out one half of dough until 1/8 inch thin on a lightly floured surface.
- Cut dough into 3-inch squares.
- Cut jalapeños in half, then in half again, until you have four similarly sized slices. Cut the slices into 1-inch portions. Pieces that are too small will be minced.
- Using one square of dough at a time, place a 1-inch slice of jalapeño in center. Top with a cube of queso blanco and finish off with a sprinkling of minced jalapeño.
- Lift right and left sides of square up and pinch together to seal. Repeat with top and bottom sides. Pinch all openings closed to seal.
- Repeat this process with remaining dough.
- Heat 1-inch of oil in a frying pan over medium-high heat. Fry poppers in batches, flipping after 30 seconds, until crispy and golden on both sides.
- With a slotted spoon remove poppers and drain on paper towels.

- Serve.

Egg Ball

Country: Guyana

Ingredients

- 1 1/2 lb cassava
- 2 tablespoon butter
- 6 eggs
- salt and black pepper
- flour
- oil for frying

Directions

- Boil cassava and 5 eggs in salted water for about 25 to 30 minutes until cassava is fork tender, drain. Mash cassava until smooth, take out the lumpy bits that cannot be mashed.
- Peel the eggs and set aside. Add 1 raw egg, butter, salt and pepper to the cassava, mix well. For egg balls, cover the eggs with the cassava to form a ball. The egg

should be completely covered by the cassava mixture. Roll in flour and fry until golden brown. Serve these with mango like chutney called 'Sours'.

Mango Sours

Ingredients

- 2 1/2 cups water
- 2 cloves finely chopped garlic
- 1 teaspoon pepper sauce
- salt and black pepper
- 2 teaspoon white vinegar

Directions

- Wash, peel and thinly slice the mangoes. Put all the ingredients into a pot and boil over medium – high heat.
- Continue to boil until everything is soft (additional water and boil longer if needed).
- Remove from fire and allow to cool. Mash with fork to combine further and add salt to taste.

Main Recipes

Buffalo Chicken and Rice Skillet

Ingredients:

- Butter spread, 1 tbsp
- Chicken breast, skinless and boneless, chopped in bite size pieces, 1 lb
- Knorr chicken flavor, 1 package
- Carrots, sliced, 1 cup
- Celery, sliced, 1 cup
- Cayenne hot sauce, 2 tbsp or to taste
- Blue cheese, crumbled, 2 tbsp

Instructions:

- Add chicken to skillet coated with melted butter and cook for about 5 minutes or until thoroughly cooked, spoon often.
- Separate and keep it aside.
- Add celery, carrots, chicken flavor alongside 2 cups of water to same skillet and prepare by following directions on the package.
- Spoon in hot sauce and chicken.
- Serve with sprinkled cheese and sliced celery (if desired).

Baked Chicken with Mustard and Lime

Ingredients:

- Chicken drumsticks, skin removed, 8
- Mustard, 3 tbsp
- Light mayonnaise, 1 tbsp
- Garlic, crushed, 1 clove
- Lime zest, squeezed, 1 lime
- Pepper, ¾ tsp
- Salt to taste
- Parsley, dried

Instructions:

- Prepare oven at 400 F.
- Rinse and eliminate fats from chicken.
- Use paper sheet to dry, arrange in a bowl and flavor with salt.
- Take a bow; add pepper, garlic, lime zest, lime juice mayonnaise, mustard and combine well.
- Put onto chicken and toss to combine.
- Add chicken to baking pan, add dried parsley topping and bake for about half an hour.
- Finish cooking for about 2-3 minutes using broiler or until golden before you serve.

Black Bean and Guac Burritos

Ingredients:

Guacamole:

- Ripe avocado, 2
- Red onion, minced, ¼ cup
- Minced cilantro, ¼ cup
- Minced garlic, 1 clove
- Salt, ¼ tsp
- Lime, 1

Burrito:

- Whole wheat flour tortillas, 2 large
- Brown rice, cooked, ½ cup
- Black beans, drained and rinsed, ½ can
- Cheddar cheese, shredded, 1/3 cup
- Lettuce, shredded, ½ cup
- Minced red onion, 3 tbsp

Instructions:

- Arrange halved avocado alongside salt, garlic, cilantro and onion in a bowl to make guacamole, squeeze 2 tbsp lime juice onto guacamole and spoon.

- Adjust seasoning.
- Scatter ¼ cup guacamole onto tortilla.
- Layer ½ rice followed by beans, cheese, lettuce and onions topping afterwards.
- Roll and pinch to close the ends.
- Add burritos seem side down in a grill pan, press with weight and let the tortilla cook for about 3-5 minutes.
- Flip over and cook for 4-5 more minutes or until golden.
- Serve alongside salsa or remaining guacamole.

Rosemary Rubbed Rib-Eye Steak Recipe

Ingredients:

- Rib-eye steaks, boneless and chopped in an inch thick pieces, 4 about 10 oz
- Salt, 1 tbsp
- Black pepper, 1 tsp
- Rosemary, thinly sliced, 2 tbsp
- Garlic powder, ¼ tsp
- Olive oil, 2 tbsp
- Butter, un-salted, 1-2 tbsp

Instructions:

- Prepare the grill.
- Take a bowl; add garlic powder, rosemary, pepper, salt and combine.
- Moisten oil onto steak.
- Add sprinkled rosemary mixture on both sides of the steak to coat.
- Grill for about 5 minutes or until medium rare.
- Flip over and grill for 5 more minutes or until medium rare.
- Let it stand for a while to cool and serve with 2 tsp butter topping.

Parmesan Crusted Chicken

Ingredients:

Breading:

- All purpose flour, ½ cup
- Eggs, 2
- Seasoned Italian breadcrumbs, 2/3 cup
- Parmigiano-Reggiano cheese, grated, 1/3 cup
- Salt, ¼ tsp
- Black pepper, ¼ tsp

- Hersbs (rosemary, chives, parsley, thyme), thinly sliced, 2 tbsp

Chicken:

- Chicken breasts, boneless and skinless, chopped in ¼ inch thick, 3-4 about 1 ½ pounds
- Black pepper and salt
- Vegetable oil, 2 tbsp
- Olive oil, 2 tbsp
- Lemon wedges

Instructions:

- Take a bowl; add flour in it.
- Add eggs to another bowl.
- Take another bowl; add sliced herbs, pepper, salt, parmesan cheese, breadcrumbs in it and combine.
- Dredge chicken (seasoned with pepper and salt) in flour and dip in chicken mixture to coat equally.
- Dredge chicken in bread crumb mixture afterwards.
- Arrange chicken breasts to a pan coated with heated oil and cook for about 3-4 minutes onto medium heat or until light brown.
- Flip over and cook for further 3-4 minutes or until golden.
- Serve alongside lemon wedges.

Chipotle Popcorn Chicken

Ingredients:

- Chicken breasts, 2
- Buttermilk, 1 cup
- Canned chipotles in adobo sauce, pureed, ½ cup
- Flour, 2 cups
- Pepper and salt
- Cilantro, sliced, 1 bunch

Instructions:

- Slice chicken breast in 1 ½ inch pieces.
- Arrange in a bowl; cover with pureed chipotle chilies and buttermilk.
- Wrap and chill overnight.
- Dredge chicken in seasoned flour and arrange in a skillet.
- Cook onto 350 F until brown.
- Season with sliced cilantro, pepper and salt before you serve.

Chicago Chicken

Ingredients:

- Jalapeno, 1
- Juice of 1 lemon about 3 tbsp
- Oregano, dried, 1 tbsp
- Olive oil, 3 tbsp
- Minced garlic, 3 cloves
- Chicken breast, skinless and boneless, 2-3

Instructions:

- Add all ingredients to food processor except chicken and process until jalapeno thinly diced.
- Put in a plastic bag alongside chicken and toss to combine.
- Let it marinate overnight, grill and serve delicious chicken.

Revolutionary Mac and Cheese

Ingredients:

- Pasta, dried, 2 cups
- Milk, 2 cups
- Cheddar cheese, loosely packed, 1 cup
- Salt, 1 tsp

- Mustard, 1 tsp

Instructions:

- Add milk alongside pasta to a skillet, bring to simmer and cook for about 20 minutes on reduced heat or until pasta softens, spoon constantly.
- (Make sure you don't boil the milk)
- Turn off the heat.
- Add salt, cheese and spoon to combine.
- Spoon in mustard and cover for about 7 minutes.
- Spoon again and serve 1 tbsp of milk (if desired).

Melt in your Mouth Chicken

Ingredients:

- Chicken breasts, skinless and boneless, 4
- Mayonnaise, 1 cup
- Parmesan cheese, ½ cup
- Seasoning salt, 1 tsp
- Black pepper, ½ tsp
- Garlic powder, 1 tsp

Instructions:

- Take a bowl; add seasonings, cheese, mayonnaise and combine.
- Scatter mixture topping onto chicken.
- Prepare oven at 375 F.
- Arrange chicken onto a baking sheet and bake for about 45 minutes or until thoroughly cooked.
- Serve hot.

Breakfast Recipes

Ham and Cheese Breakfast Sandwich with Mango Chutney

Ingredients:

- Cooking spray
- Soy ham, sliced, 8 about ½ oz
- Eggs, 4 large
- Whole-grain muffins, split and toasted, 4
- Mango chutney, 8 tsp
- Cheddar cheese, low-fat and shredded, ¾ about 3 oz

Instructions:

- Add ham to skillet coated with heated cooking spray and cook for about 2 minutes each side onto medium-high heat or until golden.
- Separate it from the pan and set aside warm.
- Recoat pan with cooking spray and cook eggs onto low heat until done.
- Arrange halved muffin upside down onto baking sheet.
- Scatter 2 tsp chutney on bottom half of muffin; add 2 slices of ham topping followed by 1 egg and 1 tbsp cheese afterwards.
- Add 2 tbsp sprinkled cheese topping onto each muffin.
- Broil for about 2 minutes or until bubbly.
- Arrange other muffin halves on to and serve.

Pumpkin Chocolate Waffles

Ingredients:

- All purpose flour, 1 ½ cups
- Sugar, 3 tbsp
- Baking powder, 1 tsp
- Baking soda, ½ tsp
- Cinnamon, ½ tsp
- Salt, 1/8 tsp
- Buttermilk, 2/3 cup

- Canned pumpkin, ½ cup (not pumpkin pie filling)
- Egg, 1 large
- Canola oil, 1 tbsp
- Vanilla extract, 1 tsp
- Semi sweet chocolate, sliced, 1/3 cup
- Cooking spray
- Chocolate shavings, sweetened whipped cream, maple syrup (to garnish)

Instructions:

- Take a bowl; add salt, cinnamon, baking soda, baking powder, sugar, all purpose flour and spoon to mix.
- Whisk together alongside vanilla extract, canola oil, egg, canned pumpkin and buttermilk.
- Spoon until properly combine and spoon in chocolate afterwards.
- Prepare waffle iron.
- Ladle 1/3 cup batter onto waffle iron coated with cooking spray, scatter and cook for about 4-5 minutes or until golden.
- Do the same with remaining batter and garnish with (chocolate shavings, sweetened whipped cream, maple syrup) before you serve.

New York Classic Breakfast Chip

Ingredients:

- Cream cheese
- Fresh dill
- Smoked salmon
- Capers
- Garlic bagel crisps

Instructions:

- Scatter cream cheese onto bagel crisps.
- Arrange fresh dill, caper and smoked salmon topping before you serve.

Banana Fritters

Ingredients:

- Ripe bananas, 6
- Beaten eggs, 2
- All purpose flour, ¾ cup
- Vegetable oil, 3 tbsp

Instructions:

- Take a bowl; add eggs, bananas and blend well.
- Spoon in flour afterwards.

- Arrange spoonful batter onto skillet coated with heated oil and cook onto reduced heat until bubbles and light brown.
- Do the same with remaining batter and let it sit in oven to keep warm.
- Serve alongside honey or maple syrup.

Best Breakfast Pancakes

Ingredients:

- All purpose flour, 1 cup (spooned and leveled in a cup)
- Baking powder, 2 tsp
- Sugar, 2 tbsp
- Salt, ½ tsp
- Egg, 1 large
- Milk, ¾ cup + 2 tbsp
- Butter, un-salted, melted and slightly cooled, 2 tbsp
- Vegetable oil

Instructions:

- Take a bowl; add salt, sugar, baking powder, flour and combine properly.
- Take another bowl; add milk, beaten egg and spoon to combine.
- Combine bother mixtures in another bowl, spoon frequently and blend properly.

- Spoon milk mixture with ingredients to until moistens with flour mixture to make batter.
- Add a bit of water if batter is too thick.
- Prepare griddle pan.
- Add ¼ cup of batter onto griddle pan coated with vegetable oil and cook onto medium heat for about 45 seconds until light brown or until bubbles.
- Flip over and cook for about half a minute or until golden.
- Serve hot.

Southern Sausage Gravy

Ingredients:

- Chicken sausage, 1 pound
- All purpose flour, ¼ cup
- Milk (2% or whole), 2 cups
- Black pepper and salt to taste
- Classic buttermilk biscuits, hot

Instructions:

- Add chunked sausages to skillet and cook until light brown.
- Add flour and cook for about a minute more.

- Spoon in milk.
- Cook until thick and bubbly, spoon constantly.
- Flavor with pepper and salt before you serve alongside biscuits.

Dessert Recipes

Orange Scented Mocha

Ingredients:

- Milk, 3 cups
- Chocolate morsels, semi-sweet, 6 oz
- Orange rind strips, 4
- Espresso, ½ tsp
- Nutmeg, 1/8 tsp
- Whipped cream sweetened
- Orange rind strips and curls (to garnish)

Instructions:

- In a saucepan; add nutmeg, espresso, rind strips, chocolate morsels, milk and cook for about 3-4 minutes or until chocolate melts.
- Turn the heat to high, spoon occasionally and cook for about 5 more minutes or until boils.

- Separate it from the heat and eliminate orange rind strips.
- Serve with whipped cream topping.

Snickers Cheesecake

Ingredients:

Crust:

- Chocolate sandwich cookies, 24
- Butter, un-salted and melted, 4 tbsp

Filling:

- Cream cheese, 3 packages about 8 oz
- Sugar, ¾ cup
- Eggs, 3 large
- Vanilla extract, 2 tsp
- Lemon juice, 1 tsp
- Cornstarch, 1 tbsp
- Snickers bars, chopped in ¼ inch slices, 3 regular size
- Caramel sauce, ¼ cup (optional)
- Salted peanuts, roasted and sliced, ¼ cup (optional)

Instructions:

- Prepare oven at 350 F.
- Add crust to food processor and blend until crushed.
- Pulse in butter and press in a pan coated with cooking spray and lined with 2 foil pieces.
- Bake for about 8-10 minutes or until firm.
- Let it stand for a while to cool.

Filling:

- Beat cheese in a bowl, add sugar to it and beat for a minute more.
- Add eggs afterwards and beat again.
- Scrape and finally beat with cornstarch, lemon juice and vanilla.
- Add sprinkled snickers onto crust.
- Bake batter arranged in water bath for about an hour or until jiggles in center.
- Separate it from the pan and eliminate foil.
- Let it stand for a while to cool.
- Wrap and chill for about 5 hours or overnight before you serve.

Applesauce Pie

Ingredients:

- Granny smith apples, peeled and sliced, 10 large
- Lemon, chopped and seeded, 1 large
- Sugar, 2 ½ cups
- Butter, 3 tbsp
- Vanilla extract, 1 tsp
- Piecrust, refrigerated, 1 package about 15 oz
- Whipped cream (optional)

Instructions:

- Add sugar, lemon, apples to a baking sheet and bake for about half an hour or until thickens, spoon occasionally.
- Separate it from the heat and throw lemon.
- Add vanilla, butter and set aside to cool.
- Follow instructions on the package to prepare piecrust.
- Put applesauce mixture onto crust.
- Roll remaining piecrust and chop in ½ inch strips.
- Place onto filling, fold and crimp.
- Prepare oven at 425 F.
- Bake for about half an hour or until light brown and serve alongside whipped cream (if desired)

Southern Sweet Potato Pie Recipe

Ingredients:

- All purpose flour, 3 tbsp
- Sugar, 1 - 2/3 cups
- Ground nutmeg, ¼ tsp
- Salt, a pinch
- Sweet potatoes, mashed, 1 cup
- Eggs, 2 large
- Light corn syrup, ¼ cup
- Butter, softened, ½ cup
- Evaporated milk, ¾ cup
- Pastry shell, un-baked, 1 about 9 inches

Instructions:

- Take a bowl; add salt, nutmeg, sugar, flour and combine.
- In another bowl; add sugar mixture alongside corn syrup, eggs, potatoes and beat.
- Slowly spoon in milk and put in pastry shell.
- Prepare oven at 350 F.
- Bake for about an hour and let it cool for an hour as well.
- Chill in refrigerator for about 3 hours before you serve.

Southern Peach Cobbler

Ingredients:

- Butter, melted, ½ cup
- Sugar, 1 cup
- Flour, 1 cup
- Baking powder, 1 ½ tsp
- Salt, 1/8 tsp
- Milk, ¾ cup
- Peaches, 3 cups

Instructions:

- Take a bowl; add salt, baking powder, flour, sugar and combine.
- Add mixture to butter and spoon in milk.
- Add splashed peaches onto batter but don't spoon.
- Prepare oven at 350 F.
- Bake in a casserole dish coated with 1 stick of melted butter and bake for about an hour before you serve.

Appetizer Recipes

Buffalo Chicken Wings

Ingredients:

- Butter, ¾ cup
- Tabasco sauce, ¾ cup
- Vinegar, 3 tbsp
- Garlic powder, 1 ½ tsp
- Sea salt, 1 tsp
- Chicken wings, 2 lbs
- Cooking oil, 1-2 tbsp
- Cayenne pepper, 1 tsp (optional)

Instructions:

- Take a bowl; add salt, garlic, powder, vinegar, tabasco, butter and combine.
- Add it to skillet and cook for about 4 minutes onto medium-low heat.
- Reserve ¼ cup sauce.
- Take a plastic bag; add sauce alongside chicken wings in bag and zip to seal.
- Let it stand in refrigerator to marinade for about 10 hours or preferably overnight.
- Prepare oven at 425 F.
- Arrange wings onto roasting pan coated with cooking oil, splash cayenne pepper (if desired) and roast for about 20 minutes.
- Flip each wing and roast for 15 more minutes.
- Add reserved sauce to coat wings and roast for further 5 minutes before you serve.

Bruschetta-Goat Cheese Cups

Ingredients:

- Crispy pastry shells, 1 package about 1.4 oz
- Goat cheese, crumbled, 1
- Sweet pepper, vegetable and olive bruschetta topping, refrigerated, 1/3 cup
- Thyme leaves (to garnish)

Instructions:

- Arrange shells in a pan, equally stuff goat cheese among them and press to flatten a bit.
- Add 1 tsp bruschetta topping onto each shell.
- Prepare oven at 350 F.
- Bake for about 4-5 minutes or until properly heated before you serve.

Caramelized Onion-Apple Bites

Ingredients:

- Butter, un-salted, 3 tbsp

- Yellow onions, finely chopped, 1 pound
- Salt, ½ tsp
- Tart apples, peeled, cored and finely chopped, 2
- Black pepper, ¼ tsp
- Puff pastry, defrosted and frozen, 1 sheet
- Fontina cheese, shredded, 3 oz
- Thyme leaves, minced, 1 tbsp

Instructions:

- Add ½ tsp salt, onion to a skillet coated with melted butter and cook for about 5 minutes onto medium-high heat or until softens.
- Add apples and spoon to coat.
- Lower the heat and cook for about half an hour or until golden, spoon occasionally. Spoon in salt and pepper.
- Keep it aside and let it cool for a while.
- Prepare oven at 375 F.
- Un-roll pastry sheet, chop, make squares and halve squares diagonally.
- Place onto baking sheet.
- Arrange spoonful apple mixture, add minced thyme and sprinkled cheese topping.
- Bake for about 18-22 minutes or until golden before you serve.

Southwest Bean Dip

Ingredients:

- Knorr vegetable recipe mix, 1 package
- Pinto beans, un-drained, 1 can about 16 oz
- Chili powder, 1 tbsp
- Green chilies, un-drained, sliced, 1 can about 4 oz
- Mexican blend cheese, distributed, 1 cup

Instructions:

- Prepare oven at 350 F.
- Add beans, chili powder, Knorr vegetable recipe mix in a blender and process until smooth.
- Spoon in ½ cup cheese as well as chilies.
- Arrange in a casserole.
- Bake for about 10 minutes, spoon and add ½ cup remaining cheese, topping.
- Bake for 15 more minutes or until thoroughly heated.
- Serve with garnished favorite taco topping.

Southern Fried Dill Pickles

Ingredients:

- Egg, 1 large
- All purpose flour, distributed, 1 1/8 cups
- Buttermilk, ½ cup
- Cornmeal, ½ cup
- Spice of your choice, 2 tbsp
- Salt, ¾ tsp
- Vegetable oil
- Dill pickle slices, 1 jar about 16 oz
- Ranch dressing for dipping

Instructions:

- Take a bowl; add ¼ tsp salt, buttermilk, ¼ cup flour, egg and combine.
- Prepare oven at 375 F.
- Use paper sheet to dry dill pickle slices, dip in butter mixture and dredge in cornmeal.
- Fry for about 3-4 minutes or until light brown.
- Use paper sheet to drain and serve alongside ranch dressing.

Disappearing Buffalo Chicken Dip

Ingredients:

- Mayonnaise, 1 cup
- Lemon juice, 1 tsp
- Cayenne pepper sauce, 1/3 cup
- Blue cheese, crumbled, ¼ cup
- Green onions, thinly sliced, 2 tbsp (optional)
- Cheddar cheese, shredded, 1 cup about 4 oz
- Chicken, cooked and shredded, 2 cups

Instructions:

- Sprinkle cayenne pepper sauce onto chicken.
- Set blue cheese aside and spoon in remaining ingredients.
- Make 1-1 ½ casserole and splash blue cheese onto it.
- Prepare oven at 375 F.
- Bake for about 15-20 minutes or until bubbles.
- Serve alongside your favorite dippers.

Kale Slaw with Apples, Cranberries and Creamy Maple

Ingredient:

Dressing:

- Vegenaise, ½ cup
- Canola oil, 2 tbsp
- Vinegar, 2 tbsp
- Maple syrup, 1 tbsp
- Pepper and salt to taste

Slaw:

- Kale salad mix, 4 oz
- Granny smith apples, sliced in ½ inch, 1 medium
- Green onion, sliced, 2
- Cranberries, dried, ½ cup
- Pumpkin seeds, (to garnish)

Instructions:

- Take a bowl; add all dressing ingredients and combine.
- Add pepper and salt to taste.
- Take another bowl; add cranberries, green onions, apples, kale and combine.
- Toss alongside dressing to coat.
- Splash pumpkin seeds topping (if desired) before you serve.

Cranberry Almond Coleslaw

Ingredients:

- Vinegar, ¼ cup
- Mustard, 2 tbsp
- Honey, 2 tbsp
- Salt, ¾ tsp
- Pepper, ¼ tsp
- Canola oil, ¼ cup
- Coleslaw mix, shredded, 2 packages about 10 oz
- Smoked almonds, sliced, 1 cup
- Cranberries, dried and sweetened, ¾ cup
- Green onions, chopped, 4
- Celery ribs, chopped, 2

Instructions:

- Take a bowl; add pepper, salt, honey, mustard, vinegar and combine.
- Slowly add oil and spoon frequently until blended.
- Take another bowl; spoon coleslaw mix with celery ribs, green onions, cranberries and smoked almonds.
- Add vinegar mixture and toss to combine before you serve.

Apple Cranberry Walnut Salad

Ingredients:

- Green salad mix, 6 cups
- Red apple, 1
- Green apple, 1
- Walnuts, roughly sliced, 1 cup
- Feta cheese, crumbled, ½ cup
- Cranberries, ½ cup

Dressing:

- Apple juice, 1 cup
- Vinegar, 4 tbsp
- Honey, 2 tbsp
- Salt, ½ tsp
- Black pepper, ¼ tsp
- Oil, ¼ cup

Instructions:

- Core and chunk apple in 1 inch pieces.
- Take a bowl; add cranberries, feta, walnuts, apples, lettuce and toss to combine.
- Take a bowl; add all dressing ingredients and whisk.
- Toss with salad to coat and serve.

Southern Chicken Salad

Ingredients:

- Canned white chicken, chunked and drained, 12.5 oz
- Boiled eggs, diced, 3
- Celery, diced, ¼ cup
- Relish, ¼ cup
- Mayonnaise, 3 tbsp
- Pepper and salt to taste

Instructions:

- Take a shallow bowl; add all ingredients together and toss to combine before you serve with your favorite crackers.

Summer Corn Salad

Ingredients:

- Whole kernel corn, thawed and frozen, 2 packages about 10 oz
- Tomato, sliced, 1 medium
- Mayonnaise, 2 tbsp
- Red onion, thinly sliced, 1/3 cup
- Lime juice, 2 tbsp
- Packed basil leaves, thinly sliced, 2 tbsp

Instructions:

- Take a bowl; add all ingredients together and combine.
- Season with pepper and salt before you serve cold.

Sweet Cabbage Salad

Ingredients:

- Cabbage, shredded, 6 cups about ½ head
- Carrot, shredded, 1 cup about 1 medium
- Green bell pepper, sliced, 1 cup about 1 medium
- Red onion, sliced, ½ cup
- Sugar, ½ cup
- White vinegar, ½ cup
- Olive oil, 2 tbsp
- Dry mustard, 1 tsp
- Celery seeds, ½ tsp
- Salt, ½ tsp

Instructions:

- Take a bowl; add red onion, green bell pepper, carrot, cabbage and toss to combine.
- Take another bowl; add sugar alongside other ingredients and combine.

- Spoon with a whisk.
- Put vinegar mixture onto cabbage mixture, toss to mix, cover and let it chill in refrigerator for about an hour before you serve.

****

Carrot cake pancakes

45 minutes - 20 pancakes - Breakfast

Ingredients:

-    1 pack of vanilla-flavored sugar
-    400 milliliter of milk
-    2 eggs
-    Butter to bake with
-    260 gram self-rising flour
-    A pinch of cinnamon
-    60 gram walnut
-    250 gram root (grated)

Topping:

-    4 tablespoons cottage cheese
-    1 tablespoon of powdered sugar

Materials

-    A mixer

Preparation:

Mix the flour with the pinch of cinnamon and vanilla sugar. Add the eggs and half of the milk.

Mix everything together and then add the rest of the milk until it is completely absorbed with the batter.

Scoop the root through the batter. Do this with all the grated root. The next step is to chop the walnuts and add it to the batter.

Heat a little butter in a pan after. After the butter is warm you need to coop small heaps of the batter into the pan.

If the underside is good brown, turn them over and bake it till the other side is also nice brown.

Mix the curd cheese with powdered sugar and serve the carrot cake pancakes with the sweet curd cheese. Finish this delicious recipe with some nuts and grated carrot.

For a healthy variant: omit the vanilla and powdered sugar

Meatball Sliders

25 minutes – 6 Meatball Sliders – Lunch

Ingredients:

- 100 gram mozzarella (grated)
- 1 tablespoon of melted butter
- 6 medium-sized meatballs
- 200 milliliter tomato sauce with herbs
- 6 small soft buns

Preparation:

Heat the oven to 180 degrees.

Do the meatballs through the tomato sauce and with the herbs. Cut the buns in half and put a meatball on each bottom half.

Sprinkle with a lot of cheese but save a bit for the topping. Put the top half on the buns and spread with a little butter and sprinkle with some cheese.

Bake the sliders in the oven for 15 minutes. Enjoy your meal! For example, eat a fresh salad as a main course.

Banana Oreo Milkshake

5 minutes – 2 Milkshakes - Desert

Ingredients

- 10 Oreo cookies

-   8 tablespoons of ice-cream
-   250 milliliter of milk
-   1 banana

Preparation

Put the milk, ice cream and the peeled banana in a blender.

Add 8 Oreo cookies in small pieces.

Mix everything fine and pour into 2 large glasses. Crumble the 2 last cookies and do it in the glasses.

CPSIA information can be obtained
at www.ICGtesting.com
Printed in the USA
BVHW090924170321
602755BV00009B/467

9 781777 624538